Acclaim for Michael Neale

"*Into the Canyon* is a stunning portrayal of love and redemption. My friend Michael Neale has written a story that has the potential to positively impact generations."

— John C. Maxwell,
Author and Speaker

"Michael Neale's *The River* gently sweeps readers along like a leaf in a current as Gabriel struggles with beginning a new life after a terrible loss. Throughout this artfully crafted story is a genuine sense of The River as a force of nature to be reckoned with, respected and learned from."

— Bookpage Review

"Neale's novel is a powerful allegory about faith in something more powerful and mysterious than oneself . . . Neale evokes a relationship between his protagonist and nature as real as any Gabriel has with the people around him as he learns that by trusting The River to guide him, he will end up where he is meant to be. The River is not without its rough patches, enabling Neale to illustrate how it is in the toughest situations that we find our way."

— Booklist Review

"Neale's novel is filled with likeable characters, and The River itself is one of them, suffused with mystery and power."

— CBA Retailers & Resources

"*The River* is a story that will transform how you see yourself and the world."

— Andy Andrews, *New York Times* bestselling author of *How Do You Kill 11 Million People?*, *The Noticer*, and *The Traveler's Gift*

"I've heard Michael Neale tell stories for years. I've been encouraged, uplifted, made to laugh, and brought to tears by them. *The River* does this and so much more. This story got ahold of me and wouldn't let go. I believe this novel will inspire many to conquer their fears, and really live!"

— Dr. J. Todd Mullins, lead
pastor of Christ Fellowship
Church in Palm Beach
Gardens, Florida

"I was deeply moved by *The River*. I found myself captured by the beauty of the story and fully immersed in the characters and their lives. I believe there's a little Gabriel Clarke in all of us. This book is a must-read for any stage of life."

— Bruce Koblish, president/CEO
of The Worship Network

"*The River* is a work of art. Michael Neale is a gifted writer. I was enthralled with every page. It gripped me and I could not put it down!"

— Lowell "Bud" Paxson, founder
of ION Television Network

OTHER BOOKS BY MICHAEL NEALE

The River

INTO THE CANYON

A RIVER NOVEL

Michael Neale

THOMAS NELSON
Since 1798

NASHVILLE   MEXICO CITY   RIO DE JANEIRO

Published in Nashville, Tennessee, by Thomas Nelson. Thomas Nelson is a registered trademark of HarperCollins Christian Publishing, Inc.

Thomas Nelson, Inc., titles may be purchased in bulk for educational, business, fund-raising, or sales promotional use. For information, please e-mail SpecialMarkets@ThomasNelson.com.

Unless otherwise noted, Scripture quotations are taken from the Holy Bible, New International Version®, NIV®. Copyright © 1973, 1978, 1984, 2011 by Biblica, Inc.™ Used by permission of Zondervan. All rights reserved worldwide. www.zondervan.com

Publisher's Note: This novel is a work of fiction. Names, characters, places, and incidents are either products of the author's imagination or used fictitiously. All characters are fictional, and any similarity to people living or dead is purely coincidental.

For information, contact: THE RIVER EXPERIENCE, LLC, 2550 Meridian Blvd, Suite 350, Franklin, TN 37067 (615) 373–2500

For bookings, contact: events@theriverexperience.com

For more information, visit www.theriverexperience.com

Library of Congress Cataloging-in-Publication Data

Neale, Michael.
  Into the canyon : a river novel / Michael Neale.
    pages cm
  ISBN 978-1-4016-8850-9 (paperback)
  1. Rivers—Fiction. 2. Guilt—Fiction. 3. Forgiveness—Fiction. I. Title.
  PS3614.E2387I58 2014
  813'.6—dc23   2014011029

Printed in the United States of America

14 15 16 17 18 19 RRD 6 5 4 3 2 1

To Bob and Bonnie Neale, my mom and dad. Words cannot fully express my love and gratitude for you both. I stand upon your shoulders in this life. You've shown me love, modeled faithfulness, and taught me the power of a committed family.

Contents

Contents

From an Entry in a Journal

So many things have happened at The River. I've loved. I've lost. I've spent. I've received. I've served. I've inflicted pain. I've run. I've laughed. I've feared. I've been at peace. I've wept. I've prayed. I've wrestled. I've lived.

Everyone longs for meaning in this life. Why are we here? What is it all about? Hope, that's what our souls need. I could not find what I needed in myself. The River gave me what I could not give myself . . . a reason.

I've seen you from afar, your waters shine and writhe.

I've heard you from the banks and beaches as you and earth collide.

I've felt you pushing, pulling, and sending over crests of waves.

I've known you truly in the deep, your arms alone to save.

The joy swallows the sorrow. To know your tears are shared is to know you have been loved.

The deepest mystery . . . The highest adventure . . . The River sweeps me off my feet . . . It leads me to serenity . . . It wrecks my plans and reminds me it is the greatest force. Never predictable but always good.

— Gabriel Clarke
November 5, 1989

Prologue

October 2, 2012, 5:00 p.m.

"Hello? Anybody here?"

I let myself in the rickety screen door. A bell over the door jingled as it slammed behind me.

"H-e-l-l-o?" Still nothing.

Behind the counter were three rugged desks with papers strewn all over them, mugs with pens in them, and a vintage rotary desk phone on the back desk. *Click. Click. Click.* Like a tired metronome, high overhead in the vaulted wood-plank ceiling, a fan made of rafting paddle blades spun slowly, moving the musty air gently in the old lodge.

It was just like I imagined it, just like he described it. The faded newspaper clippings, sepia-tone and Polaroid pictures, and tattered life vests tacked around the damp lodge entryway.

"Hello? Anyone home?"

The phone rang like a firehouse bell. No one came to answer. No answering machine. It was a Saturday evening, early October, crisp and cool. As the sun eased down behind the mountains, I walked back outside. An old army-green Jeep was parked in the gravel drive out front. A peeling bumper sticker on the back of the Jeep read "In The River." This had to be the place. The commercial rafting season must be over now. I didn't give much thought to the best time to come. I just had to find him. Things had to change for me. Maybe he would have some answers.

Across the gravel drive was a large shed with a red tin roof. The large barn door was padlocked shut. I strolled around back and the sound of the water rose. A few old kayaks were stacked on some makeshift wood scaffolding. An overturned dirty canoe lay a few feet away. I'd lived much of my life in the city. Engines, horns, sirens were the accompanying soundtracks of my days. Hundreds of thousands of people all racing after something. Even when we moved to the suburbs of Nashville, where the pace was much slower and the hay bale-covered farms went on as far as the eye could see, I couldn't seem to get the city out of me. The grind, the pace, the striving, it had a lock on my soul.

Towering trees lined the banks, forming a magical canopy. Boulders and rock formations framed the gorge, standing guard over the water. It was like something you might see in a J. R. R. Tolkien story. I sat down on a rock, took off my shoes and socks, cuffed my jeans, and lowered my feet into the frigid water. Here I was, in the middle of nowhere, Colorado. I was searching for who knows what, from a guy with whom I had only one long conversation. The water was some sort of comfort to me in that moment.

With only about thirty minutes of light left, I heard it—something banging against wood. It happened again . . . and again in a slow, steady rhythm. My city-dwelling wits told me not to venture any farther. If you go into unknown territory in the city, you are asking for trouble. But I'd traveled a long way and wasn't going to stop now.

I hiked next to The River on a moist, worn path. The sound got closer and closer. For a brief moment my mind went crazy. My respirations shot up like a sprinter.

Am I walking into a scene of a horror film?

What if there's some deranged lunatic out here?

No one even knows I'm here!

I calmed down and kept walking. Weaving through a cluster of trees, I saw someone. His back was to me. He was swinging an ax into a fallen tree. As a dead twig snapped beneath my feet, he stopped the ax at the top of his swing. He snapped his head around and looked toward me. He must have been about fifty feet away. It was nearly dark. We really couldn't see each other clearly yet. I walked a few feet closer and held up my hand in a friendly wave.

"Hey there. So sorry to bother you. I'm looking for a white-water guide named Gabriel . . . Gabriel Clarke."

No response. He turned back around and started chopping again.

I moved closer . . . slowly.

"Excuse me. Uh . . . I'm not sure if I'm at the right place. Do you know where I might find Gabriel Clarke?"

He took a couple more swings. Wood shavings flew into the air.

"Who wants to know?" the low, gruff voice responded.

"Blake. Blake Caruthers. We met in the Denver airport several months ago. He told me his story."

"A good story?" he asked as he took another powerful swing.

"I couldn't forget it, if that's what you mean," I said.

The bearded man wedged the ax blade into the wood and took off his leather work gloves one at a time. He wiped the sweat from his forehead with the sleeve of his flannel shirt as he made his way toward me.

Once he got close enough, I could see his broad, contagious smile and felt relieved.

"Blake!"

He extended his calloused right hand and pulled me in. He slapped me hard on the shoulder with his left.

"What in the world are you doing out here?"

"Not sure, to be honest." I chuckled nervously.

"Alright, then. Help me grab some of this wood and let's go grab some coffee at my cabin and we'll catch up!"

The freshly split wood smelled like a Christmas fir. Gabriel stacked a few logs on my arms and then piled several in a canvas tote that he picked up with ease.

"Follow me," he said.

"Right behind you, Gabriel."

He lumbered down a path next to The River. I kept my eyes fixed on his wool plaid shirt and knit cap as we walked deeper into the forest. It was nearly dark. The chill of the air came down on us with the moonlight. I could see my breath. The sound of the water bubbling by and the crunch of our steps was an adventurous accompaniment.

We came around a giant moss-covered boulder, much taller than both of us, and Gabriel stopped at the water's edge. He stuck his nose in the air and breathed deeply.

"Ahhh. Smell that?"

"Yes, sir. Smells like a fire burning."

"Smells like home." He pointed downstream a little ways. About one hundred yards ahead, I could see a couple of lights glowing through the window frames and a steady stream of billowing smoke illuminated by the soft light of the moon. "Pay close attention to where I put my feet. It's pretty slick. I don't want to have to pull you out of that water."

I followed closely. The path wound down around The River's edge. In a few places, we traversed over the water on fallen trees and rocks . . . not easy carrying wood. My arms were getting tired, but I would never let him know that. He had to be at least twenty years older than I was, but he was carrying twice the load. He'd made the fifteen-minute hike look easy.

He climbed the distressed wooden stairs up to the covered porch and dropped the wood out of the way.

"You can just drop it on top there. You like coffee?" Gabriel disappeared into the cabin, letting the screen door slap closed behind him.

"Sure, if you're making some for yourself." I wasn't sure if I was supposed to follow him in, so I stayed on the porch.

There were three wooden rocking chairs out there, an old barrel in the corner that served as an end table with a rack of smoking pipes perched on top, and a half-carved walking stick lying in wood shavings on the floor.

I helped myself to the middle rocking chair next to the barrel. It creaked as I settled into it, leaning my head against the tall back. The plank flooring of the porch groaned and knocked as the rocker rolled over the boards slowly. I could hear the crackle of the fire inside. The scent of smoke and cedar was deep and strong.

After a couple of quiet minutes, Gabriel appeared with two large mugs. "Cream and sugar?"

"Yeah, that's perfect. How'd you know?"

"Lucky guess."

He sat down in the rocker on the other side of the barrel. I had a flashback of him plopping down next to me in the airport, the night of our only other conversation.

"So, Blake Caruthers. What brings you all this way, man? It takes some effort to find me out here." He slurped the brew.

"Oh, I just needed to get away and thought it might be fun to track you down and hear about your latest exploits." I took a sip and shivered at its tobacco-like robust flavor.

Gabriel stared ahead at The River. Several silent seconds passed.

"I think there's more to the story than that."

I felt myself get a little nervous.

"What are you looking for?"

"Out here?"

"Yes, out here. What are you searching for?" He took another drink of his coffee and stared straight ahead.

Does he know? How could he know?

He just let me fumble over my words before it got awk-wardly quiet. I hadn't talked to anyone about what I'd been through, what I'd done. I still had walls of pride and shame built up.

"Just needed a break, maybe. I don't know if that's really important. Tell me about your last run of The River?"

Gabriel didn't let me off the hook. "How's your wife? Your kids?"

I had to catch my breath. It took me a few minutes . . . then . . . I broke. "Gone, Gabriel. She took the kids and went to stay with her mom and dad."

No response.

"She heard a voice mail on the home phone . . . from this woman . . . a woman I met on business. I moved the family south, out of the city to the suburbs. I promised her things would change, that I wouldn't work those insane hours or pick up and leave in a moment's notice."

I could barely contain my emotions.

"I wrecked my family, Gabriel. I just let it get to me, ya know? The money, the chase . . . We were young and fearless . . . We were going to conquer the world. We had everything."

I'd already said more than I wanted to. "Man, Gabriel, I'm sorry. I didn't mean to unload all that on you."

"We've all walked through the dark valleys. God knows I have."

We stared out at the water, marinating in dewy fog settling on the camp. Gabriel turned my way and broke the lull in the conversation.

"Why don't you hang out with me for a few days? I've got

an extra room here. Being out here might clear your head. A little time on The River will do you good. Of course, I might put you to work. Nothing too strenuous for a city boy."

I shook my head. I'd only come out here for some time to think and a pep talk. "I appreciate that. I've got a lot going at the office. Really busy right now."

"I see. So busy you tracked me down all the way out here, a couple thousand miles from home?"

"Touché." I shrugged.

"Come on. Trust me. The office can wait."

He smiled and held up his coffee. As we clanked our cups together to toast the moment, I felt a rising sense of hope.

The next seven days at The River changed everything.

1

The Cathedral of the Sun

March 3, 1973

"Hey!" Gabriel braked the truck at the welcome sound of his friend's voice. "I packed you something for the road."

Ezra leaned in the window and handed Gabriel a brown bag.

"You didn't have to do that, Ezra. I didn't even think you'd be awake this early."

"Cinnamon rolls, my specialty. They soothe the soul, son. And there's some hot coffee in that thermos. I even threw in a few pieces of jerky for that giant canine of yours."

Gabriel chuckled and reached over to pat Rio's head. The husky had appeared at the mention of jerky.

Ezra took off his reading glasses and let them dangle

around his neck. He squinted as he looked directly into Gabriel's eyes.

"The past colors our lives, young man, but we can't let it cripple our future. It's good to remember what's good to remember." Ezra swallowed and seemed to gather himself. "It's going to be a good day for you, son. Say hello to him for me."

Gabriel nodded and put the truck in reverse. "I'll see you tonight, Ezra."

Gabriel glimpsed Ezra in the rearview mirror. Ezra waved, then watched Gabriel drive away.

———◆———

"I don't think it's too much farther now, boy."

Gabriel's pulse quickened as the trail gradient rose sharply. With every pant, steam puffed from his eager dog. The mist was thick and the air crisp as the glow of the morning sun gradually lit up the canyon. He had never been back to retrace the steps he and his father took to Splashfire Canyon. He'd never had the courage . . . until now.

With every crunch of his boots on the terrain, Gabriel recalled memories of that fateful day. Soft flashes of scenes from his childhood emerged. Riding on his dad's shoulders, holding on to his dad's bushy blond head as they ascended the trail. He remembered hearing his father laughing. He remembered the chipmunks' chatter.

Gabriel paused for a moment to catch his breath and take in the surroundings. He looked up into the towering spruce and fir trees and then glanced back down the trail, noticing how far he'd come. A gentle breeze flowed up the trail as he drank in the morning air. He took a deep breath through his nose. Rio kept sniffing the trail ahead at least thirty yards or so; then he circled back around and playfully sprinted to Gabriel's feet.

"It's hard to believe it's been seventeen years, Rio."

Rio chomped his jaws and whined.

Seventeen years since five-year-old Gabriel witnessed that life-changing scene. Now he felt a million miles from those grief-drenched days growing up in Cairo, Kansas, with his mom. His days were hard there, but with the help of a determined single mom and some providential characters, Gabriel grew up safe and loved. The Cartwrights loved him like the best of grandparents. Miss Collingsworth knew him better than anyone, believed in him, and understood his sense of loss. His buddy Jimmy Bly looked out for him, and fittingly was the one who invited him back to experience what he was truly made for. The River never stopped calling.

Gabriel reached into his pants pocket and pulled out a twice-folded piece of paper and opened it up.

"Okay, Ezra, let's see how we are doing."

Gabriel read aloud.

"'You'll come to a fork in the trail . . . stay left.' Okay, we just did that." Gabriel glanced back down the trail. "'In about two hundred yards you'll begin to hear the falls. The trail will curve back into the woods, to the right, but don't let that fool you. Stay the course. Then it will turn back to the left, and in about five minutes you will run into a clearing overlooking Splashfire Canyon.'" Gabriel folded the paper back up and stuffed it in his pocket.

"Okay, Rio, this is it."

Gabriel took a deep breath, cinched his backpack a little tighter, and headed up the path. The smells of the forest pines were rich. As Gabriel wound his way back into the woods and then back toward the cliff on the narrow path, he could hear the roar of the cascading water in Splashfire. When he arrived at the clearing overlooking the falls, he took off his backpack and sat down on a fallen tree trunk to catch his breath. Rio sat down at attention on his hind legs facing the young man. Gabriel grabbed the fur of the dog's neck behind his ears with both hands and tussled him.

It's like this place was just waiting for me to return.

A memory played vividly in his mind's eye. He saw his father's strong right hand drawing a deep circle in the reddish-brown dirt and his left dumping the bag of marbles. The Bennington marbles donned vivid oranges, blues, and purples, clacking off of each other. He saw his father look up at him.

Ready to play? Gabriel heard it in his mind.

The sound of The River thundered in the background. The cloudy mist ascended from the falls.

Gabriel then heard the instruction of his father.

Don't go past this tree. Got it?

Gabriel walked up to the tree . . . the one he clung to as he watched his father go in after the kayaker. He leaned against it, stared down at the falls, and the memories moved faster.

Don't go, Dad! Don't go!

He heard his five-year-old's terrified self scream.

His father waving his vest, shouting, *Danger! Danger!*

The kayaker going over the falls.

4

Then—a flash of his father's hand reaching out of the torrent.

In this moment, it was like his ears closed up, the roar of The River becoming muffled. Gabriel carefully scaled down the graveled canyon wall, using the trees and rocks to brace himself. He made his way to The River's edge, just over the moss-covered boulder . . . the last place he saw his father alive.

He sat down facing the water as it powered by him, the cold spray hitting his skin as the air pushed the mist from the falls.

His heart was in his throat. A solitary droplet spilled out of his eye and down his cheek as he stared at the rushing current.

Rio joined his side as if he knew exactly what Gabriel needed in that moment.

He wiped his face on his sleeve.

"Hey, boy. It's good to remember, right? How great he was? Yeah."

Rio stopped panting for a few seconds and tipped his snout up at Gabriel. He put his arm around him.

"I had five good years with him, Rio . . . five great years." He gained his composure.

A shriek high above the canyon interrupted his thoughts. An albino red-tailed hawk floated effortlessly high overhead. Gabriel smiled as the hawk circled around the canyon for a few moments before gliding into a tree about fifty feet up the canyon wall on the other side of the water. The raptor perched at the top of a pine as if to watch the young man and his dog over the canyon.

"How about that, Rio? I think He's with us. He's still with us. Let's go, boy. There is one more place we need to visit today."

Gabriel got up and wiped the moist dirt and clay off of the back of his pants. He took his first step to climb the steep grade, back up to the clearing where he left his backpack. As he turned, he came face-to-face with a deep carving in the bark of a bright-colored silver birch tree to his left. It was a deep, squiggly horizontal line, a groove about four inches wide. He paused for a few seconds and ran his fingers over the carving.

I wonder who etched this here? What does it mean?

He continued his ascent. Rio beat him up the hill and watched from above.

"It's not fair; you have four legs!"

Rio started to bark. Gabriel glanced over his shoulder toward the object of Rio's attention. Across The River, Gabriel thought he saw a human figure slide behind a tree. His heart fluttered. He'd thought he was alone. The person was at least one hundred yards downstream so it was hard to get a good look. The bouldered terrain on the other side was rough and steep. Gabriel watched for a moment as the man wearing a black knit cap and red jacket scurried behind some more trees and then out of sight. Rio kept barking. Gabriel finished his climb up to the clearing.

Maybe it was just another hiker. Who would be this far out here and especially on that side of The River?

Gabriel was a little spooked by the experience. He always felt safe having Rio with him, though. He sat down and removed the thermos from his backpack, unscrewed the lid, and poured the piping hot brew into his favorite tin mug that Ezra had given him. He smelled the wafting fragrance of the java.

Rio started sniffing out the entire area. He zeroed in on a spot next to a stump about ten feet away and began to dig fiercely. He dug his nose in the dirt and started to sling clay out through his hind legs. Gabriel had to slide over so the flying dirt didn't hit him.

"Geez, Rio. What did you find? Is there a rib eye under there or something?"

Gabriel took another sip of his coffee.

Rio didn't come up for air. He spun around and bucked and then scratched some more. The hole was nearly a foot deep now.

Gabriel stood up and went over to see what he was after. Rio kept digging, probably after some bugs. As Gabriel got closer, he recognized something that took his breath away. Lying there at the base of the tree stump, covered in the freshly turned red dirt and clay, was a marble . . . a vintage Bennington.

Gabriel reached down and picked it up. His heart thumped as he wiped it off with his jacket sleeve. He spit on it to moisten the crustiness. It was a beautiful blue-and-green swirled marble. It had to be from the day he and his father played marbles seventeen years before.

How could it have survived all this time and stayed right here?

Gabriel was elated.

"Good boy! Good boy! Do you know what you found? A piece of history!"

Rio was oblivious as he snapped his jaws, eating the bugs in the dirt.

Gabriel held the marble tightly in his grip as he finished his coffee. He tucked the thermos in his backpack and hoisted it back on his shoulders.

He opened up his note from Ezra again. He was nervous about the next stop on his hike that day. He knew he had to go. Gabriel read Ezra's directions aloud.

"'Go back the way you came, and at the fork, take the other leg, heading up the mountain. Continue on the path for about thirty minutes. You can't miss it.'"

He folded the note back up, stuffed it in his jacket pocket, and headed out.

———◆———

Much of the trail wound its way through the forest under a canopy of juniper and fir trees. Gabriel loved the unpredictable elevation changes of the Colorado landscape. That wasn't all he loved. Every step through the woods brought back memories of his first trip back to The River with Jimmy Bly. A last-minute trip with Jimmy and his friends turned into a destiny changer for him. He thought about the stirring of the waters and his first bumbling conversations with the canyon princess, Tabitha. He could still taste that first strawberry kiss that melted his heart. Kansas—the familiarity, the safety, the comfort of what was known—held him tightly and kept him far away from his fear. It kept him from having to face the past. All that was different now. He was back—back to his roots. Back to what he was destined for. With every day, a new adventure was unfolding. He was on a quest, a quest for his soul and his purpose. Each sunrise brought fresh adversity and new opportunities for victory—victory over his anger and fear— and fresh hope for the future.

Ezra's timing was dead on. About thirty minutes into his descending hike, Gabriel rounded the last bend in the trail to a magnificent site. A vast grassy knoll that lay majestically over the calm River about fifteen feet above the water line. To the right, about one hundred yards downstream, were three giant red rock spires shooting up to the azure sky. The locals knew this formation as the Cathedral of the Sun. The gorge had an opening to the north here, and during the afternoon, the radiant light would come through the surrounding trees and illuminate the spires like a light from heaven. The shafts of light made the dust particles in the air sparkle and shimmer.

"It's just like Dad's journal described it," Gabriel said to Rio as he stood gazing, awestruck at the scenery. He had thought about coming back to Colorado several times throughout his childhood in Cairo, Kansas, especially as he got up into high school. But it was easier to not talk about it. He had pushed the bad memories down deep, until he almost forgot where he came from.

The River was wide and deep here. It moved firmly, rippling over the stones and boulders on either shore. A gentle breeze came and moved the trees as Gabriel made his way toward the giant rock formation. Rio kept pace by Gabriel's side.

About thirty feet from the base of the rocks, Gabriel unloaded his backpack slowly with his eyes fixed ahead. Rio stopped and sat at attention by the backpack, as if he knew that he was not to go any farther.

Gabriel saw the large moss-covered river stone ahead as it lay under the spires. He approached the rock slowly and knelt down. His heart raced as he ran his hand across the dirt and moss-covered etching.

John W. Clarke
1928–1956
Forever in The River

"Happy birthday, Dad. I'm sorry I didn't come sooner. It's just that . . ."

He shook his head.

"I'm back home now . . . at The River. I'm a guide, can you believe that?"

He chuckled as he wiped his eyes.

"I wouldn't even go in the water for years. I still have so much to learn, but I know it's where I'm supposed to be. I still have so many questions. I wish we could talk."

He struggled to compose himself. Rio joined him and lay down at his side with head resting against the young man's leg.

"I'll come back to visit more often, I promise. You'd be proud. I'm heading out on the water soon for a three-dayer with some of the other guides. I'm not going to lie; I'm nervous. I did my certification and everything, but I'm still not comfortable yet. I'm very much the freshman in the group. Samuel doesn't seem to have a problem with confidence. He's leading the trip. I'm not sure, but I think he has a thing for Tabitha. He doesn't seem to like the fact I'm here. Have I told you about Tabitha? Dad . . . she's perfect. She's really too good to be true. She's a huge reason I came back. I can't stop thinking about her. She makes me want to be a better man. Her dad, Jacob . . . he's an amazing dude. We're becoming close. I'm still working through things with him. I still have to fight my anger sometimes. I know he's a different guy now, but because of him, I don't have you. His other daughter, Sadie, is cute and quite a firecracker, and Freddie . . . oh, you would love Freddie . . . he's hilarious. He's dyin' for Sadie . . . or any girl, for that matter . . . to give him a shot. Love that guy." He chuckled.

He reached down to scrape a clump of dirt off of the stone and noticed another etching underneath. It was that same squiggly line he saw carved into the tree earlier that morning. The groove was deep in the stone.

"What does this mean? What do you think this is, Rio?"

Rio answered with a whimper.

Gabriel thought for a moment and then rested the marble in the center of the artwork. He stood up and took one last look at his father's grave as he brushed his hands off.

"Let's go, boy."

Gabriel turned around and was jolted by her presence. Tabitha stood a few yards away, her eyes glassy and moist. Clutching the backpack on her shoulders, she looked at Gabriel.

She walked toward him, a little out of breath from hiking, her auburn ponytail swinging.

"Ezra told me you might be up here, and I thought you might want some company. I hope it's okay that I came,"

Tabitha said. "I couldn't wait to see you." She didn't stop walking until she got to him.

He took her in his arms and hugged her close.

After a few moments they released their embrace.

"Why are you crying?" Gabriel said as he smiled.

"Because. I know . . . I know what it feels like. When Mom died, I could hardly breathe. I still remember the first time I went back to her grave by myself. It's just amazing . . . that you're here," she said tenderly as she rested her hands on his chest.

"You're the one who brought me back. That first night at The Beach, camping with the guys, then this gorgeous girl stepped out of that van. I've been captured ever since," Gabriel said.

"Oh really? What else do you remember about that trip?" she asked playfully as she dried her eyes.

"Everything," he said. "I remember what you were wearing, how your hair smelled. I remember that I couldn't sleep thinking about you. I remember when you kissed me and pulled me off the cliffs. You just seemed to know me, right away. I'd never felt that before."

"Well, I remember seeing you too. I loved the fact that you didn't have to be the center of attention. You hung back, checked everything out. I did catch you staring, though!" She laughed as she continued, "I just knew it, though. I knew you were special. That's why I kept wanting to get what was inside to come out." Tabitha patted his chest.

"It was good to come up here . . . to visit Dad. I know he would've loved you," Gabriel said.

She brushed her hair back and looked up at him intensely.

"Are you sure you're okay?" Tabitha asked.

"Yeah. Yeah, I'm good. For a second there I thought you might have been . . ."

"What?"

"Oh, nothing. Probably just some random hiker I saw across the gorge."

Rio nuzzled in between them.

"Are you okay, Rio?" Tabitha stooped and tussled the dog's fur. She looked up and caught Gabriel's eye again. "Yesterday, when you walked up and I was talking to Samuel, that wasn't anything, you know."

"We've got a trip to get ready for tomorrow, don't we?" Gabriel said.

"Yes, I can't wait."

Hand in hand, the two headed back down the path, away from the Cathedral of the Sun.

2

The First Night

Colorado

"Come on, boy! Come on!" Gabriel clapped his hands to signal to Rio that it was time to go.

The ninety-pound husky came scampering around the gear shed. In full gallop, he made a flying leap from the shore and careened into the raft, nearly knocking Gabriel into the water. Panting and slobbering with excitement, Rio tried to find his footing.

"There ya go! Good boy." Gabriel ruffled the fur on the dog's thick neck as he perched his paws on the side tube. Rio's snout in the air, taking in the view, he went back and forth between sniffing and panting.

"His eyes are just breathtaking," Tabitha said as she finished buckling her life vest. "It's like he's staring into your soul when he looks at you with those crystal blues . . . kinda like his owner." Tabitha flashed a flirty smile.

"Are you kidding me? Get a room, you two. I can't take it." Freddie rolled his eyes.

"Jealous, Splash?" Gabriel snickered from the front of the raft.

Samuel, Tabitha, and Sadie all laughed good-naturedly at the dig.

"I told you not to call me that." Without warning, Freddie "Splash" Wilburn came from the back of the raft and tackled Gabriel into the water. Rio whimpered and barked as the two wrestled in the thigh-deep water.

"Come on, Freddie! You can take him!" Sadie cupped her hands over her mouth as she continued, "Don't hurt him, Gabriel!"

Everyone knew Little Freddie was no match for Gabriel, and it was all in fun. Gabriel was well over six feet and built lean and solid, like a rugby player with broad shoulders and thick biceps. His scruffy blond beard and messy locks made him look like he was made for the mountains. Conversely, Freddy, at twenty-nine, stood a towering five feet five inches and had a slight frame, but he never let his size keep him from challenging anyone. His buzz cut made him look even smaller.

"I love it when he gets fired up," Samuel said through a grin to Tabitha. "Alright, that's enough, you two. Only a few hundred yards until the water really starts moving. Get back in here."

The serious-minded guide always tried to keep the group on track.

Gabriel chuckled as he gave one more shove to throw Freddie off of him. Freddie got his footing and stood up in the water.

"Next time, Clarke. Next time, you're mine."

This trip was a tradition before the start of every rafting season. The lead guides would come in early and head out to some of the most remote areas for a three-day camp and raft trip. It usually involved a few practical jokes, some meals by the campfire, some big white water, and most importantly, time to be with friends and prepare for the season together.

"Everything has to turn into a wrestling match with boys." Sadie finished eating her banana as the soaked guides hoisted themselves back in the boat.

"They always have something to prove, don't they?" Tabitha replied. "It's silly but it's fun to watch."

"How about a hug?" Gabriel reached for Tabitha.

"Agh! That's freezing! You are going to pay for that." She slapped him on the shoulder.

Freddie moved toward Sadie.

"Don't even think about it, Freddie." Her dark eyes flashed and she held her hand up to him like a crossing guard.

Samuel just shook his head slowly as he steered the raft downstream from his perch on the back tube. Gabriel thought Samuel looked like he might have been a Kennedy. Parted thick, dark-brown hair with graying temples. Strong, scruffy jaw.

Samuel whistled and held his hand up, motioning to Jacob who had all the gear with him in an oar raft. Coolers and camping gear all secured in faded red-and-blue dry bags were strapped down in the belly of the raft. Jacob sat perched on the rig, an oar in each hand.

"Hey-ho, here we go!" Jacob barked out his favorite saying like a marine captain.

"Hey-ho, here we go!" Their yells reverberated in the canyon.

On this particular Sunday, the sun owned the empty blue sky. Gabriel closed his eyes and soaked in its warmth, excited to begin the journey.

Sadie finished putting on the last little bit of sunscreen on her fair, freckled skin and tucked the tube back in her dry bag. The gradient in the riverbed began to drop and the current picked up. Gabriel could hear the dull roar of the rapids cascading just around the first turn.

"Okay, guys. Helmets. Lock in."

The rafters cinched their helmet straps and wedged their feet between the tubes and the canvas floor of the raft.

"Forward," Samuel called firmly.

The teams paddled slowly in unison. Gabriel sat in the bow, starboard side, with Tabitha behind him. Freddie sat in the bow, port side, with Sadie behind him. Samuel was guiding from the stern. In the briefing Jacob gave them earlier, he explained The River's CFS (cubic feet per second) was not terribly high. Only a few warm days to start the season meant the snow pack had not melted yet. This would make for some really technical rafting, which was fun for the young guides.

Jacob gripped the oars in his solo raft and called to the raft out front, "You've got some precious cargo, Samuel. Let's stay dry."

"Yes, sir," Samuel replied as Tabitha and Sadie rolled their eyes at their dad.

During the next few hours until sundown, the six adventurers enjoyed navigating a few miles of Class III and IV rapids. Winding their way farther into the wilderness, the team got caught up on their exploits in the off-season and had more than one splash fight.

The sun dipped behind the majestic mountain walls. The air cooled quickly as the moon rose to the east. The two rafts floated in a calm pool in the canyon.

"This is it, guys." Jacob led the way to a flat clearing on the shore. He jumped out of the raft in knee-deep water and muscled it up onto dry ground. He made it look easy.

"Gabriel, you wanna do the honors?" Samuel asked.

Gabriel dropped his paddle and jumped out to drag the boat onto the gravelly beach. Jacob handed out assignments.

"Gabriel, why don't you and Samuel get the fire started? Freddie, start working on the tents with me. Girls, why don't you get the food set up and prepped?"

"Women in the kitchen, huh? That's the way it always is." Tabitha bent over to loosen the strap off the first cooler.

"Woman, bring me some grub." Sadie tried to sound like her dad.

"Oh, here we go," Jacob said as he rolled his eyes.

"You can help me with the tents, Sadie!" Freddie flashed an unashamed grin.

Sadie ignored him as usual and flipped her dishwater blond ponytail over her shoulder.

Samuel and Gabriel were grabbing some large rocks to build a circular fire pit about thirty feet from the others.

"You sure you know what you are getting into with her?" Samuel asked Gabriel suddenly.

"With whom?"

"Tabitha Fielding."

"Oh, to be honest, not really." Gabriel chuckled, trying to lighten the mood.

"All you can handle, my friend."

"Oh really? How so?"

"You'll figure it out."

It was unsettling to Gabriel that Samuel was so familiar with her.

The setup continued. It only took thirty minutes and camp was in order. Three large faded orange tents, a roaring fire, strip steaks sizzling, potatoes and onions in tinfoil baking in the coals. Rio sniffed around the outer ring of the camp until he curled up near the fire, near Gabriel's tent.

The guides all enjoyed their succulent steaks under the misty moon.

"Tabitha, did you make any of that world-famous banana bread?" Samuel asked.

She was seated across the fire from Samuel, next to Gabriel. The glow of the fire flickered on her high, tan cheekbones. Her soft, auburn hair looked even more radiant in the light of the fire. She pulled her hair around her shoulder and began to stroke it downward.

"Maybe," she replied with a smile. She looked up at Samuel.

Gabriel noticed it. It was brief, but there was a definite connection in their glances toward each other.

"So, you make good banana bread?" Gabriel inquired.

"It's the only thing I can make," Tabitha replied.

"She hasn't let you taste her banana bread?" Samuel chided.

"I guess not." Gabriel looked over at Tabitha.

She stared at the fire.

"Alright, alright." Tabitha got up and walked toward the coolers on the outside edge of the camp.

"It's quite good," Samuel said to Gabriel, as if he knew something Gabriel didn't. Gabriel wasn't sure what to make of it. Suddenly, things felt a bit competitive.

Sadie noticed the exchange.

Rio perked up and put his nose in the air and began to whine.

"What's up, Rio? You smell something?" Gabriel paused, peering into the woods. "He doesn't miss anything," Gabriel said.

Rio stood up at attention and started a low rumbling growl.

Tabitha came walking back around the tents with a bag and began handing out small muffins. She noticed everyone was a little distracted at Rio's behavior.

"Did I miss something?" she asked.

"Probably just a chipmunk," Gabriel replied.

Rio stopped suddenly, licked his chops, and curled back up in his sleeping position.

Gabriel felt a twinge of jealousy when Tabitha gave the first muffin to Samuel and then began working her way around the fire.

Jacob chimed in out of the side of his mouth as he struck a match to light his pipe. "Don't forget the old and the wise over here."

While they ate, Sadie poured some hot coffee from the old black kettle. Everyone held out their tin mugs like beggars on a street corner.

"I got that kettle when you were born, Tabby." Jacob blew a plume of smoke. "That's life . . . a puff of smoke and then it's gone. Drink in the moments, kids. You think it's gonna last forever, then you wake up and you're in your fifties, contemplating the meaning of it all. I mean, right now, look at this!" Jacob held out his hands and motioned. "We are out in the wild on a perfect night with amazing food and people who love each other. The River is moving, the moon is shining, we are all healthy . . . it's just perfect. You gotta drink it in." He took a few more puffs. His tone lowered. "Just don't take it for granted. It might not always be like this."

Gabriel leaned forward, thoughtful, as the vanilla tobacco smoke floated past him.

"Dang, man, you know something we don't know?" Freddie said as he laid another log on the fire. Sparks floated into the air as the coals settled.

Jacob winked at Freddie. "I know a lot you don't know, Freddie."

Everyone laughed, and Sadie changed the topic.

"Okay, question everyone. If you could choose three different people that you would spend one day with each, who would it be? It can be anyone who has ever lived."

"Ooh, I know, I know!" Freddie raised his hand like a kid in elementary school. "Shakespeare first, then James Dean, and last but certainly not least, Raquel Welch."

Gabriel chuckled, along with everyone else.

"That was fast. Can you please explain your choices?" Sadie asked, grinning.

"Of course. I figure between the ultimate babe magnet, James Dean, and the guy who knows how to use his words to get babes, Shakespeare, they could help me know how to spend my day with Raquel!"

Freddie smiled at the chorus of laughter.

"I don't care who you pick; no one will top that!" Jacob shouted through his belly laughing.

"What? What? It makes sense, right?" Freddie swatted Gabriel on his shoulder with the back of his hand to get him to agree.

Rio began barking. At first, Gabriel thought he was just chiming in because of the laughter. But then something in his tone made Gabriel turn toward the source of Rio's frustration.

Rio faced the forest at the back of the camp on all fours, with his head down, jowls snarled, and his fur up.

Gabriel got everyone's attention. "There's definitely something out there, guys."

"Come over on this side of the fire, everyone. It's probably just a raccoon," Jacob said. "They aren't afraid to steal the food out of your hand sometimes."

Rio kept on. The forest was dense just off of the campsite. Gabriel could barely see the canyon wall rise above it just a few hundred yards in.

"Aww. Look!" Sadie pointed to her right up at the edge of the woods.

A cuddly bear cub peeked his fluffy head around the tent closest to the trees.

"That one's only a few days old," Jacob said.

Mesmerized by the little fur ball, Sadie walked slowly around the fire and got within about fifteen feet of the cub.

"Sadie, get back over here!" Jacob yelled.

"Aw, c'mon, Dad, look how cute he is."

They all saw it at once . . . like a ghost, appearing out of nowhere. The momma grizzly crashed through the trees and reared on its hind legs, roaring and swiping. Terror struck everyone's heart. The beast towered every bit of nine feet high.

Sadie froze and began to shake.

"Look down and don't talk, Sadie."

The bear lowered to all fours and began to move toward Sadie.

"Daddy!" Sadie screamed.

"Quiet, Sadie. Just back up slowly." Jacob spoke in a monotone voice and ran to the other side of the camp, waving his hands to distract the behemoth. Sweat broke out on Gabriel's forehead. No one else moved.

As she was backing up, Sadie tripped and tumbled to the ground.

The grizzly bared her teeth and unhinged her jaw in a blood-curdling roar.

Rio charged the bear, growling, but the bear lunged forward, flicking Rio away like a toy. The fierce canine yelped and landed several feet away on the ground.

While the bear was distracted, Gabriel jumped and sprinted toward Sadie. He swept the trembling girl up in his arms and ran around the back of the fire closer to the water.

The bear cub darted back into the forest, and the momma

grizzly took one more look at the campers, spun around, and lumbered back into the woods, snapping branches and small trees on her way.

Jacob ran over to Sadie and clutched her tightly. She fell apart in his arms, sobbing hysterically.

"It's okay. You're safe. You're safe," Jacob comforted.

The campers all gathered around the father and daughter. Rio came walking back over with a slight limp.

"You've got blood all over your arm," Tabitha said to Gabriel. He looked around to see where it was coming from and saw that Sadie's leg had a six-inch gash below her right calf.

Jacob's countenance wore the fact that he almost lost his daughter. "Somebody get me the first aid. We have to get this cleaned up. Gabriel, put your shirt in the water. Change it now. Now!"

Gabriel walked toward the boat to get another shirt.

"He's right. We don't want to give that bear a reason to come back," Tabitha said.

Samuel brought bandages and wrapped her wound.

Gabriel wondered if his rapid pulse would ever diminish. He expected some fun, and adventure even, but nothing this extreme. If this was just the first day, what were they in for?

3

The Stones of Remembrance

Gabriel awoke at the first signs of daybreak. It was day two of their inaugural trip to open rafting season, and the other team members were still sound asleep. It took everyone a bit to settle down the night before due to the unwelcomed visitor. In the dewy twilight, Gabriel stumbled out of his tent, donned his boots and sweatshirt, grabbed his flashlight and The Journal, and made his way to The River's edge. The water moved slowly as Gabriel sat down on a rock that jutted out over the current. The Journal had been a gift to Gabriel from his mother and contained writings and thoughts from three generations of men in his family. As he opened the leather-bound, water-stained relic, he flicked on the flashlight and began to read.

> The River—it makes, it breaks, it moves, it rests, it whispers, it shouts, it guides, it renews, it calls, it answers, it heals, it restores, it gives, it takes away, it lives.

Everything in life is a gift. Hold tight to your relationships and hold material possessions loosely. Give thanks. Gratitude is the beginning of real and lasting joy. The very breath you carry with you in your lungs is a gift from the Maker. Whether you have a lot or a little, be content. Money, possessions, power, and status are all swallowed up in The River. To love and be loved . . . that's all there is really.

1-28-46, R. A. Clarke

"What are you doing?" The soft whisper shocked Gabriel out of his meditation. He dropped the flashlight onto the rock, and it started rolling toward the water. He lunged forward onto his belly and caught it just before it fell in.

"Oh my gosh. I'm so sorry," Tabitha whispered, then chuckled.

"Are you *trying* to get my heart to stop before it's time?" Gabriel reprimanded her playfully.

She sat down beside him with her legs crossed, wrapped in her multicolored wool blanket that looked like an American Indian tapestry.

"I *was* reading, before you snuck up on me."

The glow of the rising sun was painting the canyon walls with soft light. The birds chirped in the trees, the mist began to lift, and the gorge was awakening like a flower to the sun.

Gabriel showed her the weathered book. "When my mom gave me these writings from my father and grandfather, it became one of my greatest treasures. The more I read, the more I get to know about where I came from, why I am here . . . you know . . . some of the big questions."

Tabitha leaned her head on his shoulder, and a warmth spread through Gabriel as he continued.

"I'm trying to spend my mornings reading the journal and sitting by The River. It helps me win the battles in my mind."

Tabitha turned to look into his eyes. "Ezra says some people have the deep waters in them. He says it's hard to explain, you can just tell it. Sounds like you are one of those people, Gabriel."

Tabitha looked down and read aloud.

Don't stay on the shore! Get in the waters. You can watch the waters flow from the banks, but they change you when you get in . . . all the way in. The River life . . . that's the only life for me. I eat, sleep, drink, play, laugh, live, and love, in The River! Its treasures are inexhaustible to me. This is home.

1-30-46, R. A. Clarke

"Wow, that is so beautiful," Tabitha said softly.

"Hey, remember when you were trying to get me to ride the big water with you? Your words still echo in my mind. 'You can't experience The River from the banks, Gabriel. You have to get all the way in.' . . . Remember that?"

"I said that?" Tabitha grinned.

"I guess you were pretty compelling . . . or maybe just pretty . . . Either way, it worked."

"Sweet talker."

A lisping voice broke into their romantic moment. "Is anybody cooking breakfast yet?"

"Classic Splash right there," said Gabriel.

"Why don't *you* cook, Freddie?" Tabitha craned her neck to look back at him with a little attitude.

Freddie shrugged. "I'll cook!"

Samuel came out of his tent stretching and said, "Not your gift, Freddie. Remember last time? I nearly chipped a tooth on those biscuits, and I'm pretty sure you just crushed the shells *in* with the scrambled eggs."

"Whatever." Freddie stacked wood on the fire to get it going again. There were still a few coals left simmering from the night before.

Gabriel reclined next to the fire while Jacob cooked the bacon first, then the eggs in the bacon drippings. It smelled heavenly. The coffee percolated over the open flames, and the cinnamon rolls were warming in foil on the coals.

"If it's one thing we don't skimp on, it's food," Jacob commented as he flipped the last set of frying eggs.

"I prefer to get on the water myself," Samuel said, gesturing toward the rafts.

"All happiness depends on a leisurely breakfast, Samuel," Jacob replied.

Samuel just raised his eyebrows and rolled his eyes.

"You always seem like you have somewhere to be," Sadie said to Samuel.

"We are here to run the water, right?"

"Sure, but sometimes I think you can want what's ahead so much that you miss the moments happening now. I like the moments happening now. It hurts my brain to think too much ahead." Gabriel noticed that Sadie seemed to like pushing on Samuel's driven nature.

Jacob stooped down and used a stick to stir the coals of

the fire. A log fell and sparks danced into the air. He mused as he repositioned the coals and burning embers.

"Today is always my favorite day of this trip. The next section of The River is . . . well, it's very meaningful. Gabriel, I think you will really enjoy what we get to do today."

Tabitha looked over at Gabriel and smiled.

"What is it?" Gabriel asked expectantly.

"You'll see," she replied.

Gabriel threw his hands in the air. "Aw, come on. You can't tease me like that!"

"Uh . . . yes, I can." Tabitha flashed a coy grin.

Freddie piped up, shifting his weight to one hip and moving his hands with every word. "The female species is a mystery, Gabriel. I'm telling you. They reel you in all sweetsy, sweetsy with their pretty hair, long eyelashes, and strawberry lip gloss . . . and then bam!" He slammed his right fist into his left hand. "You don't know what hit you."

All the guys started to chuckle.

"Lip gloss?" Samuel asked, puzzled but smiling.

"I do like 'em feisty, though." Freddie looked over at Sadie.

"Oh my gosh, Freddie," Sadie said, throwing her hands up in exasperation.

Gabriel joined the others as they laughed.

"I'm just sayin'." Freddie smiled.

Jacob refocused everyone. "Let's hit the water in about thirty minutes, guys."

Gabriel helped his comrades pack up the camp while the warm sun lit up the canyon sheers. He paused to admire the spring flowers. Pale evening primrose were dotted all around the beaches, bright purple arrow weed were scattered every few feet along the water's edge, and small sprigs of emory rock daisies shot out from the canyon walls and boulders. The rest of the team had already strapped the coolers and tents into the rafts by the time he refocused. They all climbed aboard the two rigs and headed out into the gentle current.

After they had been on a relatively docile section of water for nearly three hours, Jacob turned his raft facing upstream and rowed up next to the others.

"Let's go ahead and pull out here and scout the run. It's going to be a fun one."

Samuel nodded. "Not much meltdown means she is going to be extra-technical today."

"We taking a break?" Gabriel asked as they paddled to the beach.

Jacob nodded as he pulled his raft to the shore. "Why don't you come with me and Samuel, Gabriel? I want to show you how we read this run."

Jacob led the way, with Gabriel and Samuel in the back. "Put your feet where I put mine. The gravel can get really loose. That's why it's important to always be with others in the canyon and on The River. We get each other's back. Shared experiences, yes? Life is better when shared, I do believe."

Gabriel watched Jacob's climbing pattern closely as the three men scaled the rocky terrain. With every step, the sound of the water grew stronger and more thunderous.

Jacob spoke over his shoulder.

"This is probably going to be the most challenging water you've ever run, Gabe. It's pretty intense . . . but incredibly fun."

Gabriel's pulse raced. Was he really ready for this?

They exited the treed slopes and climbed out onto a flat rock that overlooked a magnificent sight. Jacob walked all the way to the edge that hung over the water at least thirty feet up. It made Gabriel nervous watching him that close to the precipice.

"Now this is white water!" Jacob's excitement was evident.

Samuel joined Jacob out on the edge. Gabriel watched from a few feet back as Samuel was pointing at different parts of The River and talking to Jacob. It was difficult to hear much of anything over the sonic wash of the water. Jacob motioned for Gabriel to come to the edge. Gabriel shuffled slowly out to meet them. Something about the water still terrified him.

At nearly a shout, Jacob began pointing things out to Gabriel. He explained the pour of the water into the falls and rapids, the shallow rocks, the logjam strainer near the end of the run, and the safest path they would take.

"You see that rock? We've gotta head into that fall from the far right or we'll get turned around and that won't be pretty." Jacob motioned with his hands.

Fear was mounting in Gabriel's chest. He hadn't done anything like this yet, not even in his training.

"You ready for Jericho Falls? Let's do this!"

The salt-and-pepper curly-headed fifty-something adventurer shouted his words, smiling from ear to ear as he pounded Gabriel on the chest.

Gabriel raised his eyebrows, nervous.

They made their way back from the twenty-minute scouting mission and loaded back into the rafts. They donned their helmets and life jackets.

"Okay, everyone, Lock in! Forward Hard!" Samuel barked the command like a drill sergeant.

Gabriel paddled fiercely, trying to stay in sync with his team. They came around the bend in The River and shot down the first rapid perfectly. But before Gabriel could blink, the next big drop was upon them. He felt the raft drop beneath them, along with his stomach. He pulled his paddle in as the team pounded into the waves at the bottom as the raft stood straight on end.

"Dig, Gabriel!" Samuel shouted.

They careened over the next few rapids as water crashed over the top of the raft. Bucking through the canyon like wild stallions, the two rafts navigated the waters exquisitely, and within just a few seconds they were drifting backward in gently moving water, facing the white water they just traversed.

"Yeah!" The soaked rafters cheered and slapped their paddles in the air.

"That was as clean of a run of Jericho as I've ever seen!" Jacob commented to Samuel.

"No thanks to Gabriel. Gabriel, you've got to keep your paddle in the water. What were you thinking?" Samuel barked.

"It was just instinct, I guess, to hold on when we went over," Gabriel said.

"Your instincts were wrong. You could've been thrown in. We've been over this. You have to pull your weight. We could've gone through sideways, and remember, your paddle in the water provides stabilization for you to actually stay in. There will be a time for us all to lean in the center, but we have to do it together. We're a team." Samuel's tone eased as he finished his rant.

"You're right, sorry," Gabriel responded.

"Don't worry, man. I've done it too." Freddie tried to comfort him.

"Samuel, you act like you've never made a mistake . . . Oh please." Tabitha came to Gabriel's defense . . . and he liked it.

He felt a little embarrassed, but the courage still came with each rapid navigated, each waterfall overcome, and each dangerous obstacle avoided.

They spun their rafts back around and headed downstream. They came around a right-hand bend in The River. The water moved firmly and smooth. Gabriel unclasped Rio's custom harness he'd made to keep the dog in the raft on sections of big water.

"There it is. I love this place," Tabitha said.

Everyone got noticeably quiet as the picturesque scene came into view. An island appeared in the middle of the waterway dividing the majestic flow in two. One-thousand-foot cliffs on either side of the waters framed the site. As they approached the serene location, Gabriel was taken by a noise he heard under the raft.

"What's that sound?" he asked Tabitha.

"What sound?"

"Listen. It sounds like . . . like marbles clacking together," he said with wonder in his voice.

"Oh yeah." Tabitha smiled. "It's river stones. The River tumbles them over and over. Over time, those rocks chip off and fall from the canyon and The River transforms them into smooth and spectacular gems."

Gabriel felt mesmerized by the gentle percussive rhythm. His mind went to his childhood and the sound the vintage marbles made when he dumped them out of the large mason jar.

Gabriel jumped out of their raft and pulled it up onto the pebbled island beach. Rio quickly followed, leaping off the front of the raft onto the shore. Gabriel helped Jacob secure his raft as well. The team members all climbed out onto the island, except Sadie.

"You doing okay?" Gabriel said, his eyebrows knitted together with concern.

Sadie nodded, but still didn't move.

"She looks really pale," Tabitha said.

Gabriel splashed back into the water. "Put your arm around my neck . . . there you go." Gabriel hoisted Sadie out of the raft and onto her feet.

Sadie sat down when they reached the shore. "Actually, I don't feel so good."

Tabitha put her hand on Sadie's forehead. "She's burning up."

Sadie swallowed hard. "I'll be okay. I'm just thirsty, I think." Gabriel grabbed his canteen from the ice chest, unscrewed the lid, and handed it to her.

"Okay, let me know if you need anything else." The older sister stroked her hair.

While Jacob sat with Sadie, the rest of the group moved away. Tabitha took Gabriel's hand and pointed ahead. "This is what I was talking about," she said to him.

Gabriel barely heard what she said. His attention was across The River.

"What is it?" Tabitha squeezed his hand.

Gabriel shook his head. "Nothing. I thought I saw something . . . someone."

"Really?"

He turned his back to her. "Probably nothing."

He glanced back one last time and saw a red jacket and knit cap disappearing into the woods several hundred yards away. His heart jumped. "Look! There! I wonder who that is?"

"Huh?" She tried to follow his gaze.

"Over there. Somebody's on the other side. I think I saw the same guy at the Cathedral."

They both strained to catch another glimpse, but there was no sign of him.

"Probably just a hiker," she said. "Come over here and check this out." She led him back across the island.

Gabriel saw a column of river rocks as tall as he was under a large cottonwood tree, each rock neatly fitted into the other, as if a mason constructed it. Rio walked ahead, sniffing the place out as usual. Gabriel approached the stone formation and noticed an etching in the lowest right-hand cornerstone.

His breath caught in his chest. It was the squiggly etching from the tree at Splashfire Canyon.

"Welcome to The Twelve Stones of Remembrance, Gabriel," Jacob said, with reverence in his voice.

4

The Symbol and Painted Words

The clouds cast giant shadows on the island as Gabriel and the others sat down in a semicircle facing the stones. The sun dipped behind the cliffs, and a soft breeze tussled Gabriel's dirty-blond, curly hair.

Jacob sat looking into the sky with his arms around his knees. "It's going to be a great night."

Jacob got up and walked with purpose over to his raft, pulling his dry bag from the stern.

"It's never exactly the same when we come here. It always changes, but it's always beautiful," Tabitha said as she gazed at the rock formation.

"Yeah, and Dad is always changing things up," Sadie remarked.

Freddie looked concerned.

"He's not going to make us sing, is he? Remember that one year?"

"A solo for you, Freddie."

"No way, you know I can't sing. I can dance. You know I can dance, but I can't sing."

Gabriel watched Tabitha as she smiled. He couldn't get over how beautiful she was.

"I don't think what you do would be considered dancing, Freddie. Convulsing, yes. Dancing, no," Sadie said.

"Aw, come on." Freddie started to move his head back and forth like an Egyptian while snapping his fingers and biting his bottom lip.

Sadie rolled her eyes.

Jacob walked up to the monument and set the backpack down. He pulled out what looked to be a small can of paint and a small paintbrush. "More on this stuff in a few minutes. Let's go ahead and get the camp set up. The tents will go on this side of the island." Jacob motioned behind him with his thumb over his shoulder. "Let's put the coolers over here, and, Gabriel, why don't you work on the fire? I'm making dinner for all of you tonight, by the way. Once we are all set up, I'll tell you a little more about the rest of the evening."

Chills ran down Gabriel's spine as Jacob talked. He wasn't sure what was ahead, but it felt important.

It didn't take them long to unload the rafts. Gabriel noticed that Sadie moved slowly but helped Tabitha set up the tents. He made a mental note to check on her later. Gabriel was able to get a roaring fire going with some dead branches and logs that lay on the beach.

Gabriel noticed Samuel kneeling down over near the water so he walked over.

"What's going on?"

"Just getting things ready for tomorrow."

"You are always thinking ahead, aren't you?"

"Just how I'm wired." Samuel used his teeth as he tied a fly lure on the line of a rod.

"You didn't have to bark at me on the boat like that," Gabriel said.

"Oh really?" Samuel looked back at him. "Pull your weight and I won't."

Samuel walked away. Gabriel got the feeling that this was about more than rafting.

Tabitha broke the tension as she called out from across the camp, "You ready for some fishing tomorrow?"

"Fishing?"

Samuel looked back, surprised at Gabriel's enthusiasm. "Yeah, you ever fly-fished?"

"No, but I *love* to fish. Mr. Earl, he was like a grandpa to me, he took me fishing in Kansas. He bought me a Zebco spincast reel for my birthday. I still remember catching my first catfish. That thing was a monster." Gabriel tried to move past their differences.

"Well, fly-fishing is a little different. Actually, it's a lot different. I'm a bit of a purest. No disrespect to Mr. Earl, but fly-fishing, it's like making art." Samuel motioned in the air as if he were revealing a painting on the wall.

"How so?"

"All of it, man. The gear, the motion of the rod and the line, the dance with those trout . . . It's just epic. Yep, my

Fenwick"—Samuel held up the rod and looked it up and down—"and my raft . . . that's all I need."

Samuel was usually a man of few words, but Gabriel had obviously touched on his passions.

Gabriel changed the subject.

"Can you tell me anything about that symbol on the rock? You know, that etching on the bottom cornerstone up there?"

"You don't know what that is?" Samuel acted puzzled as he looked up at Gabriel. "I'm surprised Tabitha hasn't told you."

"Speaking of Tabitha . . ." Gabriel looked over to make sure she couldn't hear. "Is there something . . ." Gabriel stumbled over his words.

"Is there what?" Samuel asked.

"Help!" Jacob shouted, breaking their conversation short. Samuel jumped up and ran over to the fire where a pot of stew was slipping out of Jacob's hands. He grabbed a towel and helped Jacob set the stew on the ground.

"Thanks, man. I almost lost our dinner." Jacob turned his attention to the others. "Okay, everyone . . . stew is ready!"

They all gathered a few feet from the settled blaze and sat down in their canvas folding chairs. It was nearly dark and cooling off. The light from the fire flickered on the sun-tanned faces as they waited for Jacob. He joined them with a warm smile. He looked each one of them in the eye slowly. Then he held out his hands, palms up.

"Maker, we are grateful for everything You have given. We are grateful for the waters that carry us to such a beautiful site. We are grateful for one another. We thank You for redemption. We thank You for food. We thank You for more than enough. We thank You for these moments."

Jacob turned his attention to the group.

"Go ahead and take a bowl, guys. The corn bread is in the foil warming on the coals. It's hot, so be careful. Then you can take a seat, and I'll serve you the stew."

Jacob started with Sadie.

"In The River with gratitude," he said reverently as he dipped the tin ladle in the pot and gently emptied it in Sadie's bowl.

Sadie smiled peacefully.

Each time Jacob poured the stew, he recited those words. Gabriel breathed in deeply, soaking up the sacred moment as well as the smell of broth filled with chunks of rib eye steak, carrots, potatoes, and garlic.

"Dad, this is *so* good," Tabitha commented.

Everyone chimed in.

"Amazing."

"Ridiculously good as always."

Around a mouthful of corn bread, Freddie added, "This is otherworldly, man. I'm serious . . . It's like from another planet or somethin'. It's *way* better than that pot Tabitha made last time."

"Uh, thanks a lot, Freddie!" Tabitha said.

Freddie couldn't stop. "Oh, come on. Everyone knows cooking isn't your strong suit." He chomped another bite of corn bread.

"Okay, fine, but you don't have to say it."

Everyone laughed at the hot water Freddie was getting into.

Jacob tilted his head back and focused his eyes on the starlight canopy overhead.

"You're actually not that far off, Freddie. About 'otherworldly,' that is."

"Really?"

Everyone looked at each other and wondered where Jacob was going with this.

"The world . . . the world out there has its own agenda, its own ideas of what is good and meaningful."

Jacob paused.

Gabriel jumped in. "What do you mean?"

"What do you think it means?"

"Dad never just answers the question. There's always another question," Tabitha announced with a touch of frustration in her voice.

Jacob didn't respond. He smiled.

Sadie piped up. "Yeah, Dad! Sometimes we just want to know the answer."

"Sometimes . . . we just need to *think*." He paused for a second. "Sometimes when we ask more questions and dig in for ourselves, the answers carry more weight, more richness. Sometimes it's about the process of learning."

After a few moments of silence Freddie remarked with his impeccable timing, "I'm lost."

Everybody erupted.

Gabriel said, "I think it means that what might be important to most people in the world is not really important at all in the grand scheme of things. Is that what you're saying?"

Jacob responded with another question. "What do you

think is important . . . you know, to go after . . . to set your sights on in this life?"

"A good woman!" Freddie broke them up again.

"Yes, we are well aware of your quest, Freddie." Jacob rolled his eyes. "Do I need to throw you in The River to cool off? Seriously. What about you, Samuel?"

Freddie grinned and looked at Samuel.

"Happiness and good friends," the veteran guide said decisively.

"Making great memories," Sadie said as she stared at the fire.

"Love. We should set our sights on love." Gabriel liked Tabitha's response.

"What about you?" Jacob turned the conversation to Gabriel.

"Hang on a second."

Gabriel got up and went over to his tent. He came back with The Journal.

"Most of you have seen me with this." He held up the book. "My mom gave it to me before I moved here. It's a collection of writings, journal entries from my father and grandfather, and others, I'm finding out. I just read this the other day. It's a very old entry; I'm not even sure who wrote it."

He turned so the light of the fire illuminated the pages. He read in his low, gruff voice, accompanied by the sound of the sizzling embers.

The ways of The River are pure. The River life keeps me about the right things. Away from The River, it's a lifeless desert to me. Away from The River, I hear, "Climb! Power!

More power!" while The River life whispers, "Kneel. Help. Serve." Away from The River, I try to control, but in The River, open hands are the answer. Away from The River, I hear, "Repay! Revenge!" and The River life proclaims, "Let go and be free!" Come to The River. In The River, there is always more than enough.

A hush came over the group as Gabriel finished. He closed the antique leather-bound collection of writings.

"I don't think I am anywhere close to this yet. But it seems like a great place to be."

"Wow. I don't think I could say it any better."

Jacob got up and went over to the remembrance monument and took out the parchment paper he had placed there before dinner.

"Everyone gets two sheets of paper."

He walked around the fire passing them out. Then he went back over and picked up the cans and the brushes. He passed them out without saying a word. When he was finished, he stood in front of the monument facing the team and the fire.

"The story goes like this. In the late seventeenth century, a beautiful and radiant Cherokee Indian woman named Ama-Woya, which means 'Water Dove,' was taken by a group of ruthless and violent men. Plucked from her tribe in what is now the Carolinas, this young woman made the trek all the way to Colorado as a slave to these three depraved settlers. They abused her in every deplorable way.

"One night at their camp, as the men were in a drunken stupor, she managed to escape by way of The River. She made her way along the water's edge with only the moonlight and the sound of the waters to guide her."

Gabriel leaned forward, elbows on his knees, eyes intent on Jacob.

"She was willing to risk everything, even her own life, to taste freedom. She lived off the land for days. Day and night, night and day, she trekked through the wild terrain, and at one point could only traverse a part of the canyon by giving herself over to The River. She surrendered to the current that night. It took her through huge rapids and over treacherous waterfalls. Miraculously, she survived. Gashed by a river rock, she was left with a deep scar on her right shoulder."

Jacob made his way over and knelt down at the corner of the monument. He put his hand on the etching that Gabriel was asking Samuel about before.

"Gabriel, this is the image of the scar of Ama-Woya."

Gabriel's thoughts whirled. *This is unbelievable. How did this symbol get to that tree at Splashfire where my dad died? Or to his gravestone? To this monument?*

"This crude marking, this squiggly line, this is a symbol of The River."

Jacob ran his finger in the etched crevice. His tone became more hushed and reverent.

"Ama-Woya used this symbol to remember that The River was her only way out of slavery. She would carve this symbol everywhere she could to declare The River had saved her. The River set her free."

Gabriel sat silent as he churned on the deep memories of his father's death. The fact that his father died saving the

storyteller in front of him was something he was still working through. Day by day, wrestling through his respect and
love for Jacob, yet dealing with the anger he carried for so
long. Then it entered Gabriel's mind just as Jacob spoke up.

"Strangely familiar, isn't it?" Jacob pulled up his sleeve,
showing the horrific scar he suffered on that fateful day.

It looks just like the etchings . . . the symbol of Ama-Woya!
Gabriel stared in disbelief.

Jacob lightly ran his fingers over his healed wound.

"Remember, this scar has a name . . . Mercy. The River
had mercy on me that day. It had mercy on me in my stu-
pidity and arrogance. It had mercy on me through your dad,
Gabriel."

For once, Gabriel couldn't meet Jacob's eyes as his filled
with tears.

"One day, a few months after the accident, I went back
to visit the site where it all happened. I found this rock on
the side of the mountain just above the falls at Splashfire."
Jacob pointed to the cornerstone with the etching. "Most
people would say this needs to be in a museum, but I think
it needs to be right here." He continued, "I showed it to Ezra.
He actually knew the story of Ama-Woya. Every year for the
past seventeen years I have brought a stone here, to honor
the memory of your father and to honor The River. I call it
The Stones of Remembrance because I don't ever want to
forget what was done for me. I don't ever want to forget what
I live for. The scar was a symbol of freedom for Ama-Woya,
and these stones are a symbol of freedom for me."

Jacob's voice quivered as he looked the stack of stones
up and down, running his hands over them.

"Storms have come and the water has risen, but surprisingly, it's never been washed away."

Gabriel had so many questions flying through his mind. Before he could choose which one to ask, Jacob turned the conversation over to Tabitha.

"Tabby, why don't you explain what's next."

"Okay, guys, it's time for us to each add a stone of remembrance ourselves. Take a minute to find a rock, at least this size." She held out her hands about the size of a loaf of bread.

"Go on." She motioned to get them moving. "Come back here when you've found your rock."

After a few minutes they all settled back around the fire with their rocks. Freddie had one he could barely carry.

"As we all know, it's Gabriel's year, he's the rookie. Each one of you will go to the monument with your rock. Take the brush and dip it into the can of red paint. On the rock, each of us will paint one word, a description of something that we see in Gabriel."

Gabriel took a deep breath. Tabitha went on.

"These words are meant to speak of the life we see in Gabriel. Then place the rock of remembrance on the wall as a symbol of his life in The River."

She looked into Gabriel's eyes with deep intensity.

"Gabriel, when we are finished, you paint your word to The River and place it on top."

Over the next several minutes, one by one, each team member painted, and the rocks went up.

Tabitha went first.

Courage

Sadie . . .

Rescuer

Freddie . . .

Friend

Samuel . . .

Guide

As the firelight flickered against their faces and on the monument, Gabriel's eyes welled as he took in these words. It was as if they were painted on his soul. Jacob was the only one left to go. He painted slowly and then hoisted his large rock on top of the others. The smack of the rock echoed in the canyon. Jacob dusted his hands off and then wiped his tears on his sleeve. His swollen, wet eyes met Gabriel's focused stare. Nothing was said. Jacob walked back over to his place by the fire. Gabriel stared at the word, feeling unworthy.

Hero

"That is who you are." Jacob sat down.

"I don't know what to say, guys. I mean . . ." Gabriel shook his head, overwhelmed by their kindness. For the first time in a long time, he felt hope for the future lifting him over his sadness from the past.

"It's all in you, Gabriel. It's all in you . . . because The River is in you," Jacob said.

Gabriel took his rock up to the monument, his hand shaking as he dipped the brush in the thick red paint. He inscribed in big bold letters . . .

GRATEFUL

5

Bones

Lying on his back, zipped up in his sleeping bag to his scruffy, bearded chin, Gabriel awakened slowly to an arresting aroma floating past his nostrils. The smell of syrup and bacon was the very best way to wake up. Enjoying the fact that there was no set time to start the day, he turned over to his side and fluffed his makeshift pillow of two old sweatshirts. While trying to doze back into his blissful state, he heard a familiar voice humming by the fire. His curiosity got the best of him, so he unzipped his tent, propped up on his elbows, and poked his head out to a wonderful surprise.

"Hungry?" The white-haired, dark-skinned elder raised his eyebrows as he lowered the large iron skillet on the coals.

Rio jumped up from his slumber and came over to give

Gabriel a good-morning face lick. Gabriel was unphased as he pushed Rio's snout to the side.

"Ezra! What are you doing here?" Gabriel smiled.

"I'm cookin'," Ezra said matter-of-factly.

"How'd you get over here?"

Gabriel got out of the tent in his faded, navy-hooded sweatshirt and stumbled as he shoehorned his hiking boots on with his fingers.

"I have my ways."

Ezra, from the very beginning of Gabriel's journey back to The River, was a light for Gabriel's path. Talking to Ezra, for Gabriel, was a window into his dimly lit childhood. A great friend to his grandfather and a mentor to his father, Ezra knew The River well. His wisdom helped Gabriel continually wrestle and untangle the grief and fear that shaped his broken childhood.

"What are you cooking? It smells amazing." Gabriel leaned over the skillet and fanned the air up to his nose.

"Caramel apple skillet bread with a side of sugar-cured bacon and some coffee."

Ezra stayed busy laying strips of thick-cut bacon on another iron skillet that rested on the cooking grate. He pulled his hand away quickly each time as they sizzled and popped spitting grease into the air.

Gabriel got a towel and used it to grab the coffeepot from off the grate. He poured a cup of the steaming black brew. He settled back into his canvas chair.

"Last night was amazing, Ezra."

"Tell me about it."

"We talked about The Stones of Remembrance. I heard

about Ama-Woya. I think that was her name. I want to know more about her . . . and the symbol. Something tells me you've got more scenes to that story in you."

Gabriel pointed to the stones with the painted words.

"And up there, that was incredible. I've never felt anything like that before. I could barely sleep thinking about it all."

"It's good to remember what's good to remember." He smiled gently as he commented through his low, Southern Louisiana gate, "New stories now, Gabriel. New stories." He stayed focused on flipping the bacon.

"What do you mean?"

"The pen is in your hand. Every conversation, every adventure, every relationship . . . That's right . . . new stories. And now that you're at The River, your story is going to come alive in new ways. Every day is a blank page. You can choose to keep writing the past or you can write something new. That's what The River gives us, new blank pages and the backdrop for the extraordinary to happen."

Ezra looked up and squinted as the sky brightened by the second.

"I just don't want to screw it up . . . I'm not much of a writer and there're lots of pages that have already been written. It's kind of easy to write what's already been . . . and then read it over and over and over." Gabriel stayed with the metaphor as he rotated his hand in a circle.

"It's worth the risk. I could have made my famous cinnamon rolls and that would have been good, right?" Gabriel nodded. "But you got to step out." Ezra reached down and scooped out a piece of the caramel apple bread. "Here, try this."

Gabriel took the spoon. He blew on it to cool it off.

"Oh. My. Gosh. That is heaven." Gabriel mumbled through his chewing.

"See, a new story."

"Hey, save me some!" Tabitha's voice behind them startled Gabriel.

She leaned over and wrapped her arms around his shoulders. His heart raced, surprised by her open display of affection.

"Not a chance." Gabriel took another lick of the spoon.

As her hair fell on his cheek, Gabriel caught a whiff of cinnamon. At that moment, he wanted to sweep her up, carry her away, and spend the day together. Instead, he lightly squeezed her arms in return.

She stood up, walked over to Ezra, and gave him a kiss on the cheek.

"How's my favorite chef in the whole world?"

"Better now," the old man chimed.

One by one the others woke and joined them by the fire. After eating their fill of breakfast, they packed up the rafts. Jacob and Ezra headed out first. Everyone but Gabriel was in the raft.

"Gabriel, you coming?" Freddie yelled out.

"Be right there."

Gabriel stood at The Stones of Remembrance one last time. He bowed his head for a few silent moments. He put his ball cap on, his dirty-blond hair pouring out of it. He walked back to the raft slowly with a sense of great peace. Freddie patted Gabriel on the shoulder as he approached the raft.

"Five bucks says I catch more fish than you today."

"Oh really?" Gabriel chuckled.

Freddie kept going. "I hope you were praying up at the stones just now . . . praying for fish. 'Cause you're gonna need it."

Rio was the last to jump in the raft as they pushed off the island and into the gentle current. Samuel piped up as he sat on his lead guide perch on the back tube of the raft. "Freddie, have you even caught a fish here before?"

"Tons! You watch."

Tabitha turned to Gabriel. "Ezra *always* catches the most fish. I don't know how he does it, but he does . . . every time."

Samuel responded with a smile. "I think he puts some kind of potion on his flies to put a spell on the trout."

The five rafters entered the center of the current and the boat picked up a gentle speed, floating through the canyon like a magic carpet. Feeling the cool morning air awaken his senses, Gabriel loved the feeling of the water patting the bottom of his feet in the occasional gentle bubbling rapids. He was a million miles from his fear of the water as a child back in Kansas. He felt truly free.

Straight ahead downstream, The River seemed to dead-end as it made a sharp turn to the right. The gradient steepened a bit and the white water churned.

"Nothing too crazy here, guys, but we need to enter over to the left beyond that big rock." Samuel's tone was firm as he motioned with his left hand. "Right forward."

The boat spun left.

"All forward."

Everyone paddled in unison. The raft picked up speed as they descended with the water. Up and down they splashed.

"Forward hard!"

Samuel could see they needed a little more power to make the turn and reach around the left side of the boulder. The right side poured into a suckhole that didn't need to be traversed. Everyone dug in. The back right side, where Samuel sat, just clipped the boulder and slung the back of the boat around as they cascaded around the rock. They careened through the next couple of rapids backward and spun back around downstream.

"Come on, guys. That was pathetic," Samuel barked. His brow furrowed. "If we are going to ride the really big stuff at the end of the day, we have to be sharp on the little stuff."

Sadie tightened her ponytail and looked off in the distance.

"How are you feeling?" Tabitha seemed concerned.

"Fine."

"Something's on your mind."

"Later."

"How's the leg?"

"It still hurts pretty bad."

Gabriel noticed Ezra first and pointed at him. "No way!"

Standing about ten feet from the shore, Ezra stood in The River knee-deep in his waders. He had his tan-colored fishing hat on with a smile the size of Texas. Cradled in both hands was a fish.

"Woo-hoo!"

Tabitha slapped Gabriel on the arm. "I told you!"

"How'd he get here?"

"Ezra knows all the forgotten trails of the canyon."

"I guess he does." Gabriel investigated the canyon with his eyes to see which way was plausible for the old man.

The River forked here. To the left, The River was deep, wide, and smooth. To the right, the waters cascaded gently through some spectacular rock formations. The sun bounced off the shiny rocks and sparkled in the waving waters. There were small babbling rapids and pour-overs that fed pristine swirling eddies, a perfect spot for fly-fishing.

"What did you get?" Samuel asked as they pulled the boat closer.

"A tailwater rainbow!" Ezra held it up. His grin didn't fade a bit.

The beautiful fish wiggled in his hands. It was silver-green with black spots and bright fuchsia painted down each side.

Jacob was on the bank putting on his waders.

"I'm still tying my fly on and Ezra already has one bagged!"

Ezra lowered the foot-long trout back in the stream gently. They all watched it wriggle free and disappear into the stream.

Ezra shook his hands to get the excess water off of them.

"Look at that little guy. He's a living work of art. Endless treasures in these waters . . . endless treasures."

"I'm fishing with Ezra," Gabriel declared as he jumped out to pull the raft up on the shore.

"You can if you want, but I'm telling you, if a fish has a choice between your fly and Ezra's, he will pick Ezra's every time," Samuel said.

Ezra smiled at Samuel as he pulled a piece of jerky out of his vest pocket and tossed it in his mouth.

They all disembarked. Freddie started passing out the waders.

"I think I'm just going to read today," Tabitha said. "I'll leave some of the fish for you boys."

"I'm fishing," Sadie said emphatically as she took the smallest pair of waders from Freddie. "It'll take my mind off of my leg maybe."

Samuel pulled the rods out of the boat and handed one to Gabriel. "Here, this is yours. Be careful with it. It's a vintage Fenwick."

"He's pretty precious about his fishing stuff," Sadie quipped.

Samuel paid no attention as he was sliding on his waders.

"I'm going downstream. I'll catch all of the ones you guys miss." Freddie headed out.

Rio bounded all over the beach, sniffing every rock.

Tabitha settled in with her book on the beach. Samuel and Sadie each found spots downstream a bit where they could cast. Jacob came over and joined Gabriel and Ezra.

"I've never fly-fished, so I'm going to need some help, guys," Gabriel said.

"You're a natural at everything. You'll do great," Tabitha mentioned, looking over her book.

"Watch Ezra. He is an artist." Jacob motioned his head toward Ezra as he waded over next to Gabriel.

Ezra paid no attention as he began to cast his line.

"He doesn't force it. He has a rhythm to his cast. You see he doesn't break his wrist very much. It's all one fluid motion.

He takes the tip of the rod to ten o'clock and two o'clock every time."

Jacob showed Gabriel the basics of holding the rod, loading the line, and the trajectory of the fly. Gabriel hung on every word. It brought back memories of his very first catch, a huge catfish in a river at the southern border of Kansas. It was the trip with Mr. Earl, the old man who owned the farm in Cairo, Kansas, where he and his mom rented a room.

"You want to set that fly down on the water just like a real river fly. Those trout are finicky, so how you land them is important. It takes time to learn, so be patient. Once you get it, you'll love it," Jacob instructed.

Ezra's rod bent into a rainbow shape.

"Here we go! Come to Uncle E, fishy. Come to Uncle E!"

Jacob waded to shore quickly to grab the small fishing net and threw it to Gabriel.

"Scoop him up!"

Ezra dragged the fish in closer and guided the rod over toward Gabriel.

"Wow!"

Gabriel reached to get the net under what looked to be a huge multicolored trout. "Look at that whale! Only you, Ezra!"

"Uh-huh. Yep, she's a few pounds, that one is." Ezra grunted as he struggled with the fish, trying to get it close enough so Gabriel could capture it.

"Reach and get him! That fly isn't going to hold!" Jacob waded back into the water to join them.

"Al-most . . ." Ezra strained.

Just then Ezra's rod snapped straight up in the air and the line whipped in the wind.

"No! Gabriel, you've gotta move quicker, man!" Jacob said.

They all just looked at each other, stunned that they lost the giant trout.

"I'm so sorry, Ezra. Dang it!" Gabriel slapped the water.

Ezra shrugged and smiled. "Oh, that's alright. I'll catch her again."

Before they could sulk too long, Rio captured their attention. His aggressive barking echoed through the canyon. They turned to see the wolf-like dog about twenty feet up the mountainside. All that was showing was his hindquarters jutting out from behind a rock. He was scratching and digging in the reddish dirt violently. He sprayed the pebbles and dirt between his back legs.

Tabitha put her book down.

"What did you find, Rio?" Tabitha started to climb up the uneven terrain, placing her palms on the rocks to secure each step.

"Be careful," Gabriel said protectively.

"She's a climber. She knows what she's doing," Jacob remarked.

While the men were focused on getting their lines in the water, Gabriel turned and noticed Tabitha's reaction. Her hands went up, cupped over her mouth and nose.

"What is it, Tabitha?"

"Oh my God. Come up here!" She motioned to him frantically. "Oh my God!" She said it again through her hands.

Rio was still barking and digging frantically.

Everyone got out of the water quickly. Jacob and Gabriel made it up the hill first. They approached the girl and the dog. Tabitha turned away.

A dirty white skull, now half covered, lay faceup in the clay, only a few teeth left in the small jaw. Another small six-inch bone and some smaller ones lay uncovered as well.

"Rio, get back." Gabriel pulled the dog back by the collar as he licked his chops and stomped nervously.

Gabriel's heart was in his throat. Jacob leaned down to get a closer look.

"That's a child . . . a very small child."

A glorious morning of fishing and frivolity turned quickly into a morbid discovery. Rio had uncovered some kind of tragedy. Gabriel felt nauseous as they stared silently.

6

The Agents and the Scene

9:30 p.m.—Big Water Adventure Camp

Thunder rattled the frame walls of the camp lodge and lightning sparked all through the canyon. It lit up the dining room like a shorting strobe light.

"It's comin' down now," Ezra said as the white noise of the rain pelting the tin roof of the old building grew louder. He stood at the large copper sink drying the last of the dishes. He never stopped working until he found his rocking chair at the end of the day. The team returned from their three-day trip, which had the most bizarre of endings. Recovering from unpacking all the gear, they relaxed into the evening.

"Hot cider?" Ezra offered mugs to Gabriel and Tabitha who were seated at the long rough-hewn spruce dining table.

"Sure," Tabitha answered as she laid the quilt over Sadie's legs.

"How's your leg?" Tabitha asked her younger sister.

"Hurts."

"Sadie, do we need to take you to the doctor?"

"No, no, I'm fine, really. Just need to rest, I'm sure."

Tabitha smiled and patted her sister's shoulder.

"Gabriel?" Ezra motioned to him with a mug.

"No, thank you."

"You sure? It'll warm you up," Ezra said.

Gabriel broke his distant furrowed stare, shaking his head to acknowledge him. He'd lost his appetite for anything. He couldn't help but think about the last scene of the trip . . . the bones.

Jacob, hands in the pockets of his faded jeans, gazed out of the large sixteen-pane window watching the rain blow sideways. The old rotary phone rang out at the front desk. He looked toward the phone before he spoke. "I'll bet that's the sheriff's office."

He took a sip of his cider and walked out briskly, his boots rumbling the plank wood flooring with every step.

"Big Water," Jacob answered shortly.

Ezra stopped putting away the dishes so everyone could hear Jacob's conversation.

"Yeah . . . Yeah, Steve. We were fishing at the fork just below the Cathedral and our dog went exploring up the hillside . . . Yeah, and he started barkin' and diggin' like crazy. We went up to see what he'd found and it just took us all off guard."

Jacob glanced back into the dining area as he continued

in a somber tone. "Yeah . . . Uh-huh. I'm no expert, but I'm pretty sure it was a small child. We saw the storm was coming in, so we threw a tarp over the bones and secured them with some tent pegs."

Jacob lowered his voice. The others couldn't make out what he was saying. They all looked at each other. Then Jacob signed off. "Okay, Steve. I'll see you in the morning."

Jacob hung up the phone and walked back to the dining room with his cider, shaking his head.

"What are they going to do?" Sadie asked.

"The storm is too bad to head out there tonight so he wants me to show them the site in the morning."

"I want to go." Gabriel surprised even himself with his quick response.

Jacob nodded. "Meet me at the Jeep at six thirty sharp."

Ezra put the last dish away, draped his towel on the sink, and walked toward the door slowly. He grabbed an old trash bag out of the cupboard and draped it over his head.

"Ezra, you're going to get soaked," Tabatha said. "You don't have to go home tonight. We have room for you here."

The old man looked over at her, his countenance weighed down.

"Sometimes things aren't as they seem. You just never know what you'll see when you come to The River. Good night, kids. "

He walked out into the torrential rain.

After a few seconds of silence, Gabriel looked at the girls, puzzled. "What did that mean?"

Tabatha shrugged her shoulders, but Sadie spoke up.

"I'm not always sure with Ezra. When he speaks, it always seems like there's more than one thing he's actually saying."

Gabriel looked over at Jacob, hoping for some more explanation.

The lightning flashed relentlessly.

"How are reservations looking for opening week?" Jacob asked as he rinsed out his mug.

"It's actually filling up quite nicely," Sadie piped in.

It wasn't lost on Gabriel that Jacob changed the subject.

"It's hard to believe the season is on us already. Seems like just yesterday you joined us." The veteran guide looked over at Gabriel as he continued. "The rest of the guides come in next week, and we'll do your final swift-water rescue certification. Then the week after that we are all in."

Gabriel sat staring at the table, tracing the knots in the wood with his finger. Earlier today he'd been looking forward to this season. But now . . . he wasn't sure why, but he felt a shadow hanging over him.

"I wonder if it was a boy or a girl," he said almost to himself.

"Ugh . . . I'd rather not think about it . . . It's just so sad." Sadie shivered.

"I guess we'll find all that out soon enough," Gabriel said.

———◦◉◦———

"Glad I put the top on before it started to pour yesterday. I can't believe it's still coming down," Jacob said as he and Gabriel got in the old Jeep and rambled out the gravel drive of the camp. The jerky windshield wipers squeaked with each swipe of the glass, and the headlights were so dim that Gabriel could only see about twenty feet ahead of them. They were supposed to meet the police at the site where they found the bones in one hour. It would take them every bit of that to get there.

"Hey, did you happen to grab any tools from the gear shed in the recent past?" Jacob asked.

"No, why?" Gabriel replied.

"Just curious." Jacob had a puzzled look. "I'm missing some of my best tools. I can't remember when we had any theft problems around here. It's just odd."

"I haven't seen anything."

Gabriel sipped some coffee from his thermos.

"Do you still love it?"

"What's that?"

"The River. Being at The River."

"Absolutely." Jacob paused and then glanced over at Gabriel. "You're not having second thoughts on me, are you?"

Gabriel didn't answer right away. He stared out his window.

"I don't think so. No."

"A bad day on The River is still better than the best day anywhere else."

"You sure about that?" Gabriel raised his bushy blond eyebrows. "Being at The River seems to carry its share of pain."

The Jeep chugged as Jacob downshifted through another set of switchbacks.

"You're right. Pain comes to all of us . . . there's no escaping it."

Gabriel shook his head, lost in his thoughts. "Whoever lost that little baby probably wants to escape it."

Jacob looked a little surprised. "I know. But you can't escape it. You have to go through it. That's the only way."

"I'd prefer to escape it, thank you very much."

"Wouldn't we all," Jacob replied.

Something triggered in Gabriel and he exploded. "Do you even know what it's like to walk through that kind of loss?"

Jacob furrowed his brow and cocked his head.

"Well . . . uh . . . I'm not sure what to say. Are you okay? What's going on?" Jacob asked.

"I'm just not interested in hearing how to deal with something from you." Gabriel looked out his window.

"Um. Okay." Jacob backed off, and for a while they rode in silence.

"Okay, I think we're getting close." Jacob wiped the condensation from the inside of the windshield with the back of his hand.

"Why?" Gabriel resurrected the previous conversation.

"Why what?"

"Why do we have to go through it?"

"Here we are." Jacob hit the brakes and made a right turn off the main road onto a path that led through the dense area of forest. "It's part of this life, I guess."

The Jeep bounced through the rough terrain for about fifteen minutes, hitting muddy holes and crunching over dead branches.

"A lot of pain we experience seems to be caused by other people's choices." Gabriel looked straight ahead.

There was no time for Jacob to respond. They pulled up to the clearing to see another Jeep Wrangler, this one was black with a sheriff's emblem on the side. Parked next to it was a mud-covered white Jeep Wagoneer with a government seal painted on the door.

"Looks like the Feds are here too," Jacob said as he shut the engine off and secured the parking break. The steady rain pelted the canvas roof of the Jeep.

Jacob and Gabriel flipped up the hoods of their rain jackets and exited the vehicle. Jacob waved at the two men seated in the local sheriff's Jeep.

"The tall guy with the crew cut, built like a lineman, is the sheriff, Steve Carrington," Jacob said. "Jack Ballard is a plainclothes detective who has been on the job for nearly thirty-five years. I've known both of them for a while."

Gabriel nodded, but his mind couldn't focus on the two men. He felt nervous to see the bones again, yet compelled to do it at the same time.

As they approached the group, one of the federal agents stuck out a hand toward Jacob. "I'm Special Agent Fowler; this is Special Agent Brighton."

They all exchanged handshakes and introductions. Gabriel thought that Agent Fowler looked more like a well-groomed middle-aged businessman than an FBI field op. Agent Brighton had a firm handshake, dark hair pulled back in a bun, and she wore no makeup.

Jacob looked down at the FBI agents' outfits. He spoke up loudly as the rain was beginning to come down harder.

"It's a bit of a hike from here, maybe twenty minutes or so. It's going be slick because of the rain, so be careful. You got any boots you can wear?"

"We'll be fine," agent Brighton said, gripping the small sifting box.

"At least you have pants on," Jacob said, smiling.

She did not seem amused.

"You sifting for gold?" Jack chuckled at his own question.

The sheriff broke in. "We aren't getting any drier. Show us the way." Steve motioned to Jacob.

Jacob and Gabriel went out in front and the others followed close behind. They traversed through misty forest on a muddy path. They wound around giant boulders and through towering trees. Jacob and Gabriel glanced back every few minutes to make sure the officers were with them.

Occasionally, Jacob would call out cues. "Here's where we descend a bit. It's slick."

Jacob and Gabriel went first, bracing themselves on the rocks, slipping intermittently as the wet clay gave way under their boots. The local officers stayed close behind and the FBI agents behind them. After descending about thirty feet or so, they came to a level clearing. Agent Brighton was moving slower and was still up the hill a ways.

"Be careful!" Jacob cupped his hands over his mouth to project his voice over the rain.

As soon as the words left Jacob's mouth, Agent Brighton left her feet. She dropped to her backside and started sliding. She careened over a couple of small rocks and tore the back of her pants halfway up her thigh. By the time she came to a stop, red mud covered every inch of her.

The men all scrambled to help her.

She held up her hand, looking embarrassed, and stated emphatically, "I'm fine. I'm fine." She got up, holding the flap of torn material back to her leg.

"I've got some tape up in the Jeep if you need it," Steve said, averting his eyes from her bare leg.

"Thank you, Sheriff, but I'll manage," she replied with a tinge of disgust.

"I told her she didn't need to come out here. She's a rookie," Agent Fowler mumbled to Gabriel.

Now that they'd confirmed the agent was alright, Gabriel wanted to get back to hiking. "Wasn't it right over there?" Gabriel asked Jacob, pointing across the hill.

Gabriel started walking toward the large boulder. *It's gone!* He spun around looking everywhere. *How could that have happened?*

"This is exactly where it was." Gabriel pointed to a large mud puddle that had formed in the clay.

"That's what I thought," Jacob commented as he walked over to Gabriel. Both men looked all over the area.

Gabriel held one arm straight toward the water. "We were fishing right there. This is the only rock like this around here. The bones, the tarp, it's all gone."

"Gentlemen, what's going on here? I got up at three a.m. and drove three hours for this?" Agent Fowler's tone turned condescending.

"I'm telling you. This is where the skull was, and there were other bones as well . . . lying right here." Gabriel motioned, his heart racing.

"Look!" Gabriel crouched and pointed to a couple of smaller holes. "This *was* it. Those are from the pegs we hammered to hold the tarp."

Jacob knelt next to Gabriel. "The wind would not have been strong enough to pick that up."

"You sure?" Agent Brighton agent asked.

"I'm sure." Gabriel noticed Jacob sounded irritated, something that rarely happened.

Gabriel splashed some of the water out of the hole and scraped up some of the mud. "It's pretty deep now, deeper than what Rio did. I think somebody dug them up."

Agent Fowler grabbed the small spade he brought. He dug around the area and dumped the mud into the small sifting box. Agent Brighton sifted through the clay, assisted by Gabriel, for a half an hour, but to no avail.

"There are no prints, no tracks, nothing thanks to this rain." The sheriff got up and brushed the clay from his knees. "I'm done."

The rain finally let up a little as they made the arduous climb back to their vehicles.

"If you see or hear anything, don't hesitate to give me a call." Agent Fowler handed Jacob and Gabriel his card.

Gabriel was still trying to make sense of everything. "I'm just curious. Are there any open cases regarding missing children in this area?"

"Yes, unfortunately," the agent responded. "Let me know if something comes up."

The two agents loaded in their Wagoneer and motored off.

Just then, an alert came over the two-way radio in Steve's Jeep.

"Carrington, come in, over." The static made it difficult to understand.

The sheriff leaned into the vehicle. "This is Carrington."

"We've got a drunken disorderly at the diner, assistance needed."

"Jack and I are on it. Over."

Steve turned his attention to Jacob. "Let me know if anything comes up."

Gabriel and Jacob got in the Jeep and started the journey back to camp.

For a while, neither spoke. But frustration got the best of Gabriel, and he suddenly slapped the dashboard in anger. "Who in the world would have come out here between yesterday evening and this morning in the pouring rain to dig up those bones? Who even knew they were there?"

Jacob shrugged, unphased by Gabriel's outburst. "Somebody must have been watching us. That's the only way."

Gabriel's mind immediately flashed back. "I haven't thought too much about it, but you remember when I went back to Splashfire, to visit my dad's grave?"

"Yeah."

"While I was down at the falls, I caught a glimpse of some guy leaving the woods on the other side of The River. It was like he was sneaking away."

"What did he look like?"

"All I could see was his red jacket and black knit cap. It was spooky. Just the two of us out there and he didn't say a word. He just scooted off into the woods like a hunted animal. Tabitha saw him that day too. And then I saw him again while we were camping along The River."

Jacob didn't reply. He looked into the rearview mirror. Without warning he cut the wheel sharply to the left across the road and slid to a halt. He executed a three-point turn on the narrow road and sped back the way they came.

"Where're we going?" Gabriel asked, nervous.

"I want to check something out." Jacob's tone was perturbed, almost angry.

"Is it about the bones?"

"I don't know. Maybe."

7

Billy

After a twenty-minute drive of steep switchbacks, Jacob downshifted the Jeep as he rumbled off the road onto an unmarked path.

"So you never said where we are going," Gabriel said, still feeling trepidation. He was trying to read Jacob, but his normally calm demeanor was intense and concerned.

Jacob didn't take his eyes off the road, but he frowned. "I'm not totally sure. I saw a truck turn off here a few weeks ago. I've never seen anything or anyone coming in or out of here before, and what you said just got me thinking."

They wound through the trees on the uneven path and to the precipice of a steep and rocky descent. Jacob stopped the Jeep abruptly and pulled the parking break. He stepped out and locked the wheel hubs, then jumped back in and jammed the shifter of the old CJ-7 into four-wheel drive.

They actually leaned back in their seats, the path was so steep. The Jeep rocked back and forth as it traversed the rocks and potholes like a mountain mule. After about two hundred yards, the path leveled and turned to the right. As they made the turn, Gabriel saw a small, rustic cabin.

"Somebody lives down here?" Gabriel noticed smoke coming from the other side of the cabin.

A frown still creased Jacob's forehead. "Looks like it."

The sun was beaming, not a cloud in the sky, but the forest was so dense here it felt like the evening twilight.

A couple of old, faded green kayaks were lying in some overgrown brush at the base of some large firs next to the cabin. The red tin roof had pine needles, moss, and twigs strewn about on it. The small front deck had a lone rocking chair with a couple of kayak paddles leaned up against it.

As Gabriel and Jacob got out of the Jeep, a few tiny chipmunks scampered out of a stack of two old truck tires lying to the right. Gabriel heard the rushing of the white water that was close but out of sight. The two men walked up onto the small wooden porch. Jacob dropped his sunglasses around his neck and banged on the door hard.

No answer.

"Anyone home?" Jacob called.

Still nothing.

Jacob seemed troubled, as if he knew something about this, but Gabriel didn't feel like he could ask any questions yet.

Jacob started to walk around back. Gabriel cupped his hands and took a peek in the dirty window. He could barely make out a small wooden dining table with a couple of chairs. A couple of books lay on the table next to what looked to be a leather-covered flask of some sort. He couldn't see much else. He followed Jacob around to the back. There he saw a fifty-five gallon, rusted-out barrel still smoldering and spitting smoke from some debris that was burning.

Some old tools lay up against the back of the house: a pickaxe, a shovel, and a wood splitting maul.

Jacob rattled the back door. It was open. He stuck just his head inside.

"Hello?"

Still no response.

"I'll be right back." Jacob eased himself inside, but Gabriel couldn't do it. This place just didn't feel right to him.

After a few seconds that seemed like hours, Jacob returned from checking out the one-room cabin.

"No one here. Let's go."

Jacob pulled the door closed and led the way. As soon as Jacob made the turn around the corner, Gabriel heard another voice.

"What are you doing here?" The slurred growl was venomous. Gabriel turned just in time to see a tall, wiry man with a shaggy beard charge at Jacob in a full sprint. Jacob quickly stepped to the side, deflected the blow, and the man fell hard into the dirt.

"Easy, man, easy." Jacob held up his hands toward the man.

Gabriel wasn't sure what to do. The two men stared at each other, circling like wrestlers in a ring.

The tall, wiry, drunken man wiped his mouth. His faded denim shirt, torn jeans, and boots were covered in mud, and it looked like he hadn't slept for days.

"Why can't you leave me be?" he slurred angrily.

Gabriel watched, shocked, Jacob's face paled, and his mouth dropped open.

"Billy? Is . . . is that you?" Jacob squinted as he stared.

The man waved wildly at them. "Get off my property!"

"I thought you were dead!" Jacob shook his head. "Where have you been?"

Suddenly, the man seemed calmer. "Billy? Billy? Oh, he's dead . . . he's been dead for years."

Jacob looked confused. "How did he die, then?"

"Who's the pretty boy with you?" The drunk ignored Jacob's question and pointed at Gabriel. "What are you doing here?" he yelled, but Gabriel stayed quiet.

The man pulled a large hunting knife out of his boot and pointed it straight at Jacob. His veins in his neck pulsed as his face burned red with anger.

"I'm done talking!"

"Okay. Okay." Jacob held up his hands again and then motioned to Gabriel.

The two men backed up toward their Jeep.

The man kept the knife pointed at them, but it shook as he tried to keep it straight.

"Another time, Billy; it's okay."

Jacob and Gabriel got in the Jeep. They didn't speak as they made the rocky descent back out onto the main road.

Jacob slammed his hand on the steering wheel. He was mumbling under his breath.

"Who was that guy?" Gabriel finally asked.

Jacob stared ahead as he drove. His demeanor looked shaken. "I . . . I haven't seen him in a long time. I thought he was dead." Jacob pushed his right hand through his salt-and-pepper curly hair. "I tried to find him for years. He's going to kill himself if he doesn't stop."

Gabriel puzzled over this information. "Have you known him long?"

Tears welled up in Jacob's eyes. "All my life."

Gabriel felt a shock like electricity run through his body. "You are related?"

Jacob nodded. "That's . . . that's my little brother." He took a breath and paused, seeming hesitant. "He disappeared after . . . He's had a rough time, a really rough time . . . more than his share of tragedy. I know everyone has some suffering, some tragedy in life . . . but for some, it seems to overwhelm and get the best of them. God, he looked terrible."

Gabriel didn't know what to say. His bushy blond hair blew in the wind as he processed what he saw and heard.

"Are you going to try again?" Gabriel looked over at Jacob.

Jacob took a shaky breath. "I have to. Unfortunately, there's a lot more to this story that I can't talk about right now. Hopefully Billy will come home. I want him to come home. There is life after mistakes. Everyone has a past. But everyone has to choose. He has to choose life." Jacob gripped the steering wheel with both hands. "I hope he chooses life."

———◈———

Jacob dropped Gabriel off at the lodge and drove away, saying he needed some time to think.

Gabriel paused on the porch, running his fingers through

his hair. He felt overwhelmed by what had happened during the last twenty-four hours. Surely he was due for a break by now.

He glanced in the lodge window before he opened the door, and what he saw made his heart stop—Tabitha, a steaming mug in both hands, gazing up at Samuel, his hand in her hair.

Gabriel's eyes narrowed. *What is going on?* He threw open the lodge door, making Tabitha and Samuel both jump.

Tabitha stood up from her chair, smiling awkwardly. "Oh, Gabriel! Hi! How did it go?"

Gabriel ignored her question.

Tabitha put her mug down and walked toward him. "Whatever you think is going on, isn't. I had a leaf in my hair, and Samuel was getting it out."

Samuel stomped toward the door, slamming it behind him.

Gabriel didn't know what to think.

Tabitha pulled him into her arms, but he didn't return her embrace.

"Gabriel, listen to me. There is some history with Samuel. We are just friends. Honest. Samuel wanted more, but I didn't. I see him like an older brother. Which is definitely *not* how I see you." She reached up and ran her fingers through his hair, and Gabriel felt his anger softening.

"Join me for some tea?" she asked.

A few moments later, they were both settled on the couch, sipping tea.

"So, tell me how this morning was with the sheriff," Tabitha said.

As Gabriel filled her in, her eyes widened with shock. A few moments passed.

"I can't help it. I just keep wondering what happened. Why here?" Tabitha's tone escalated. "Who could've done such a thing? I wonder how long ago it happened."

Gabriel didn't have an answer for her.

Tabitha eventually continued, "It's interesting that we ended up here at The River. I could have grown up in Chicago or Georgia or somewhere. Colorado is all I've really known. Sometimes I wonder . . . I don't know . . . if there's more out there. I wonder what I'm missing." Before Gabriel could respond, she kept going. "You didn't hear me say that . . . Dad would lose it."

He paused for a moment. "I've often wondered the same thing, how we all ended up here. And I don't know what life would have had for you in Georgia, but I can say this with absolute certainty: I don't want you to be anywhere but here."

She smiled and laid her head down on his shoulder. "I know you've had a lot of loss in your life, Gabriel, but I'm not going anywhere. You're stuck with me. Never worry about that."

8

Gabriel's Cabin

October 2, 2012, 8:15 p.m., Gabriel's Cabin

"You're like a moth to a flame with that thing."

Gabriel caught me checking to see if I'd gotten any messages or e-mails on my phone at the first lull in the conversation.

"It makes your face glow and everything," he said, nodding at the phone.

"Habit, I guess."

There was not one bar of service out in the wilderness. I felt pretty stupid as I put it back in my jacket pocket. Where the airport conversation left off, the conversation at the cabin picked up. The adventure seemed palpable. It was a welcome distraction to my own misery. I still had so many questions.

What happened to Tabitha? Did he marry her? What about the bones? Where is Jacob now? Or Billy?

"You hungry?" The early-sixties mountain man dumped the last bit of coffee over the railing.

"Actually, yeah, I am," I replied.

"Let's head back up to the lodge. I've got some steaks in the fridge up there that are begging to be grilled over the open flame."

"Oh, man, you don't have to go to any trouble. We can just go to a restaurant or something."

Gabriel looked at me and chuckled. "There's a diner in town, but if I were you, I'd have one of my steaks." He smiled. "Besides, preparing a meal for a friend is a privilege."

"Okay, sounds great. Just didn't want you to go to any hassle."

Gabriel set the coffeepot down on the ledge. He slid his arms into the sleeves of his flannel overshirt.

"Serving others isn't a hassle. It's a joy. Come on. Let's go eat." He lifted his eyebrows and smiled as he started down the steps of the porch. I followed.

Gabriel seemed to have a view of life that flew in the face of everything I'd been about. I'd spent my life climbing the proverbial ladder. It almost seemed as if everything up to this moment had been a blur, another rung to climb and another hill to conquer, another investment to discover. I'd reached all my goals—money—and lots of it, cars, a second home—I was a pacesetter in the financial district. So here I was, hanging out with a mountain man, searching for God knows what in the wilderness. The irony wasn't lost on me. By all normal measures, from the outside, I was a successful investment banker. Deep in my gut, though, I felt like a street beggar.

We made the short hike along The River back up to the lodge. The air chilled quickly in the canyon after the sun ducked behind the mountains.

I helped Gabriel get the charcoals going on the large, brick grill pit out on the edge of the deck. I looked around and imagined some of the scenes Gabriel had told me about tonight and when we were in the airport together. I imagined Jacob Fielding giving his famous opening season speech as the torches flickered. I pictured all the young apprentice guides carousing and enjoying the food. I thought about the old man, Ezra, who made cinnamon rolls and dispensed his otherworldly wisdom. I felt like I was on the set of a thirty-year-old movie. The characters and dialogue were vivid in my imagination

Gabriel lit a few of the oil torches to shed some light. We sat down at one of the weathered picnic tables on the deck. He slapped down two ice-cold soda bottles with one hand. The spread was enormous for just two people.

"Gabriel, this looks incredible. You always eat like this?" I looked down at the feast of rolls, grilled potatoes, three bigger-than-your-face rib eyes, salad, and sliced tomatoes. The aroma from the juicy, charred steaks was straight out of heaven.

"I try to," he said as he grinned. He reached over and twisted off the soda bottle caps like they were toys. He handed me one as he held his up for a toast. He looked up to the sky and surprised me with what he said.

"Maker, we are thankful for more than enough. We are

thankful for Your River. We are thankful for mercy. We are thankful for friends. May we give as You have given, love as You have loved."

He looked back at me and held up his bottle.

"To great friends, great food, and great white water."

"Hear, hear." As our bottles clanked together, I felt mysteriously connected to the moment and to this guide. I'm not sure why, but it felt familiar and right. I'd only known him for a few short hours in two separate conversations nearly a year apart, but I felt like I'd known him for years.

"Now this is a steak knife!" I said through a laugh as I held up the twelve-inch serrated blade.

Gabriel smiled as he cut into the sizzling meat. "So, tell me about your family."

"I have three kids . . . two crazy boys and a girl in between."

"What are their names?"

"Jake is my oldest. He's sixteen. Lily is thirteen. She's my princess. Dylan is the little firecracker. He's six."

When I said my kids' names, I felt great happiness at the thought of their faces, but the stronger feeling in that moment was sadness . . . deep sadness. I'd failed them. I couldn't be with them and it was killing me.

"You miss them." Gabriel took another bite and squinted as he focused on me. The food looked and smelled amazing, but now my appetite was dwindling, and I idly pushed salad around on my plate.

"More than I can say, really. Jake is driving now . . . and life is all about girls and sports. Lily has these deep dimples when she smiles . . . melts me every time. And Dylan is always looking for something to jump off of. These gray hairs all have that one's name on them."

Gabriel laughed.

"I've got to figure something out." I felt and heard the desperation in my voice. "Sarah was a senior in college when we met. I had already been working in New York for a couple of years. One weekend I dropped in to surprise my sister at her college campus, and Sarah was her roommate that semester. She was stunning. She still is. She's actually smarter than she is pretty, which is dangerous. She can hold her own in any debate too. Once I met her, it was like I didn't have a choice. Like I was supposed to marry her from the beginning of time."

Gabriel nodded thoughtfully. "How do you think it happened?"

"What do you mean?"

"How did you drift apart?"

"I don't know where it started, really. I was hoping you could tell me," I said, suddenly nervous. "I think it's the natural way . . . you know, to drift away from each other."

"You think it's supposed to be that way?"

"I didn't say that. I just said it seems to be the natural way of things . . . to come apart . . . to get weaker . . . We lose sight of things. It takes extraordinary effort to keep things right . . . to keep people together. Left alone, we wander. I don't think she appreciated all that I was doing for her and the kids. I worked my butt off, fourteen-hour days for years to get us where we were."

"And where was that?" He smiled graciously.

I didn't have an answer. Then it hit me.

"How could I spend my life chasing after everything that *doesn't* matter? I hate losing. It's like someone moved the goalpost or something! I don't know what to strive for anymore."

I was hoping he would give me a glimmer of hope. As we took the last few bites of the incredible meal, Gabriel got up to take the dishes inside. "I have an idea," he said as he rubbed his hands together, chewing the last of his dinner roll.

"What's that?"

He held up his hand as he swallowed.

"I'll be right back." He had that crazed look in his eye I remembered from the airport.

He came out of the kitchen and walked past me with a purpose.

"Let's go."

"Go where? It's got to be closing in on ten o'clock."

He looked back over his shoulder at me.

"You got somewhere to be? Just come with me. You'll see."

I followed him across the gravel drive. He took me down to an old wooden barn-like structure. He unlatched the large door and swung it open. It smelled of rubber, river water, and a touch of mildew. He pointed over to the wall.

"Flick that light on, will ya?"

I turned the light on to see a row of hundreds of wetsuits hanging high on a rack like suits of armor, a large wooden crate of helmets, stacks of wetsuit booties, and rows of life vests all sorted by size. Gabriel picked one off of the "large" rack and tossed it to me.

"That should fit."

"What do I need this for?"

"Always wear a vest on the white water, my friend."

"What? We don't need to go out on the water."

He walked right over to me. His presence was powerful.

"Really? I beg to differ. That's why you came, isn't it? To get in The River?"

I stumbled over words. "Well, I just wanted to . . . you know . . . get a change of pace."

He smiled and lowered his voice a bit. "The River *is* the change of pace. I'm going . . . and you're going with me."

He smiled again as he pushed a paddle into my chest.

I didn't have a choice. I fancied myself a pretty adventurous guy. After all, I was an avid runner. Being on The River at night took it to another level.

"I'm not really dressed for this."

"The River doesn't care how you look," he retorted quickly. "Put on the wetsuit, grab a brain bucket, and meet me at the Jeep," he commanded as he walked out of the barn carrying his gear.

I stood there, half angry, but half excited. I was going on The River at night with a notorious adventure monger.

I hollered after him, "Am I supposed to wear this wetsuit over my jeans?"

"I wouldn't do that. You want to keep the moisture away from your body."

"Uh . . . okay." I'd have to strip down to my boxers and T-shirt. *What in the world am I doing?*

After I gathered the gear, I trudged back out to the parking area. I stopped by my brand-new black BMW 740i sedan to drop my leather dress shoes in the trunk and grab my sneakers. It seemed odd to me. This dream car didn't seem to mean much out in the wilderness.

I helped Gabriel hook up the trailer to his Jeep. It carried the raft and had a large white cooler strapped to the back. After a few minutes' ride through the canyon switching back and forth, we pulled into a small clearing, and Gabriel backed the trailer down to the water's edge.

The next thing I knew, I was in a raft on a mighty river with Gabriel Clarke, floating into a moonlit canyon in Colorado. You could say I was officially out of my comfort zone. What a far cry from my office at 590 Madison Avenue in Manhattan. Once I got over the shock of what I was doing, I came awake to the experience.

A starlight canopy twinkled above. All I could hear were the sounds of the water. In the distance you could hear the dull roar of rapids. Up close, just the occasional bubbling of the gentle flow over the riverbed rocks. The moonlight beamed, but the occasional cloud would block its light, rendering the canyon pitch-black for a few seconds. I felt the water tap the bottom of my feet as we coasted along, Gabriel in back, and me in front on the starboard side.

Smack! Smack! Smack!

"You hear that?" Gabriel asked as we floated along.

"Yeah, what was that?"

"Beaver tails. They're warning everyone of the city dweller."

I laughed.

Then a coyote howled high in the hills. It was a chilling sound.

"Go ahead and get secure. Slide your foot under the tube there, and when I say 'forward hard' or 'backward hard,' you dig into the water. That will steady you in the boat. This next rapid will be fun in the dark."

I could feel my adrenaline pulse as I braced for my first ever white-water experience. The night made the water seem infinitely strong and mysterious. I could barely see the water, but I could hear the roar get louder. I paddled furiously, not knowing if I was helping or doing the right thing. The raft picked up speed. It felt like a cosmic invisible rope was pulling us faster and faster toward something. Gabriel guided us from the back, steering us between boulders and over the waves.

"Forward hard!" he yelled several times. My heart pounded as I connected with the water. It splashed my face. It awakened my senses. I felt like a child again, scared and thrilled at the wonder of the moment. We cascaded over a small drop, and I felt the boat turn quickly. We were now floating backward.

"Forward hard! Hard!" Gabriel yelled. I thought we were in trouble. The raft bucked up and down.

Gabriel and I dug in as we pulled the raft upstream against the rapid. Then suddenly we felt the struggle release and we just floated, pointing upstream, the boiling waters cascading all around us. The moonlight beamed onto the white water we now faced.

"We're surfin' now! Ha ha!" Gabriel shouted.

It was a magical experience. It was as though the waters allowed this peaceful respite in the middle of the raging water. We stayed there for a minute or so, and Gabriel backed us out into the flow, and we headed downstream once again.

"Have you ever been over a waterfall?" he asked as we paddled gently.

"What?"

I'm sure he sensed my fear.

"I'm just kidding. Did you enjoy that little run?"

"Yeah, it was amazing. Little?"

"Yeah, that was only a level two. I'll take you on a four plus tomorrow."

I didn't want to let on that I was really nervous at such a prospect.

"Okay. I wasn't sure how long I was going to stay."

"One of the things I love about these waters is that just when you think you can't handle any more big white water, she blesses you with a section like this. Look around."

We pulled up our paddles. The water here was pure peace. The River opened wide as if to invite us into its tranquility. The mirrored surface reflected the moon's brilliance, and the roar of the white water melted into deafening stillness. I leaned over the side of the raft and I could see my reflection in the smooth and dimly lit surface. The dark outline of the mountaintops that surrounded us looked like someone drew them in charcoal on the canvas of the sky. A hawk screeched and the cry reverberated. I was in another world. It was like one part of me started to die and one part of me started to awaken from the dead. It was just nature and us . . . no deadlines, no big business deals, and no media. I was in the presence of power and beauty, and I felt very small.

"Stunning," I commented to Gabriel as I looked up to the sky.

"It's in the dark that I hear the waters differently. When I can't see, when I don't know, when it's hard, that's when I listen. Life becomes clearer when I have to trust . . . trust that it's going to be good . . . in the end, it will all be good. When I come to The River, I'm actually the truest version of myself. I think that's because I realize it's not about me."

Gabriel's words burrowed deep into my soul. Could it be good again for me? I was hoping beyond hope.

9

The Reflecting Pool

1973

The match flared as Gabriel struck it against the box. He lit the kerosene lantern and hung it under the rail of the porch. The rocking chair outside his cabin room, adjacent to Ezra's, was his favorite place to read at night. The River coasted along just a few feet away. It bubbled and washed over the bedrock, creating a lush and unceasing natural accompaniment in the wilderness.

Gabriel turned the lamp key a quarter of a turn to brighten the light and opened The Journal to read.

> I often wonder where I'd be without The River. At some
> point, I'm not sure when, it became the center. I want
> to know the waters. I want to hear the waters . . . not

just hear, but also listen. I want to feel the waves and the eddies, the peace and power, the current and the calm. I knew of the waters for years. I'd heard stories about people taking trips and riding the white water, but once I experienced it for myself, it changed everything. I know people who are near the water, but they don't embrace it. Whether fear or indifference, they have never allowed themselves to be swept away. My family tree is forever changed. I hope I'm around to see my children's children embrace The River. The River washed away my past. New beginnings is the theme of these waters . . . new beginnings.

R. Allen Clarke,
June 23, 1946

"Hey!"

A hushed shout erupted from the darkness beside the porch. Gabriel jumped to attention and dropped The Journal as he looked into the woods.

He heard snickering as he saw two figures dart off behind the trees.

"Hey, who's there? Freddie! Was that you? You're going to pay for that!" Gabriel shouted through a whisper so he wouldn't disturb Ezra, who had already turned in for the night.

Gabriel looked down at Rio. "I thought you were supposed to protect this place?" The dog lifted his eyes but stayed comfortably curled up in his sleeping position.

"Were you in on it?" Gabriel asked the lazy dog again as he sat back down, his pulse still racing from the prank.

"Whatcha doin'?" Tabitha startled him as she came up the steps from the other side of the porch.

"Are you kidding me?" Gabriel leaned back in his rocker and closed his eyes and exhaled.

"What?" she asked with a puzzled tone.

"Your timing is impeccable. I just got scared out of my boots from this side and then you get me from over here." Gabriel motioned to both sides of the porch.

Tabitha plopped down in Ezra's rocking chair.

"Was it Freddie?"

"Probably. He's going to pay."

Tabitha bit her bottom lip as she smiled from ear to ear.

"It was you, wasn't it?"

"I would never," she said through her Cheshire cat grin.

"Aw, man." Gabriel shook his head in disbelief.

Tabitha stood up in front of Gabriel and pushed her knees between his. Her faded jade-green sweatshirt matched her eyes. Her form-fitting, faded Levi jeans had a hole in the left thigh revealing her tan skin. She leaned down and put her hands on the rocking chair arms, her face just inches from his.

"Come walk with me."

Her breath smelled like spearmint. Gabriel was nervous but exhilarated. Their eyes locked.

Before he could respond, she grabbed his hands and pulled him up.

"Okay, okay." Gabriel reached inside the door of his room and grabbed his flashlight. They descended the steps of the porch and followed the path at the water's edge. This time they headed upstream.

They held hands on the rocky path that weaved through the towering pines and firs. The narrow beam of the flashlight shook along the path in front of them. After a few minutes hike, they arrived at a clearing next to some gentle rapids.

"Let me see the flashlight." She dropped Gabriel's hand and shined the light on a series of rocks that led out into the flowing water. One by one, she hopped and stepped her way on each one until she landed on the last one big enough to sit on. It was about thirty feet offshore and smack in the middle of the light rapids. Gabriel stood alone on the banks.

"Uh, I can't see anything."

Tabitha shined the light back on Gabriel's feet, then on the first rock in front of him.

"Come on out!" she yelled. "Just follow the light. It's easy."

Gabriel didn't reply. He took the first step and held his arms out to catch his balance.

He lifted up his large hiking boots to take his second step, and the light moved. His foot landed on the rock, but he was disoriented by the darkness and almost fell in.

Tabitha started laughing. "I'm sorry! I sneezed!" she said over the sound of the waters.

"Keep it steady please!" Gabriel said through a smile. This moment was another picture of their brief journey together. It was Tabitha pulling him, calling him into something new and beautiful. She was the risk taker; he was trying to find his way. She seemed to know him better than he knew himself.

He hopped his way over each stepping-stone to join her

in the middle of The River. The couple sat side by side facing downstream, the waters rolling by on both sides.

"Are you glad you came?" Tabitha asked as she leaned on his shoulder and slipped her right arm through his left, clutching his bicep.

"Where, out here?"

"Well, yeah, but I mean out west, to Colorado, to The River?"

"You ask a lot of questions." Gabriel stared ahead for a few seconds before he continued. "I'm really glad I came to The River but . . ."

"But what?"

"Nothing . . . not important, really," Gabriel said.

"I'd like it if you'd tell me. I wonder about stuff too, ya know? I've grown up here. It's all I've known. I often wonder if I'm missing something out there. I feel like there's more, but I'm not sure what. How could I want something different from this amazing place, ya know? Why do we always want what we can't have?" Tabitha looked off in the distance. "I'm not sure if the proverbial grass is greener, but sometimes I just want to see it for myself."

"I'm still working through some stuff, that's all."

"What kind of stuff?" Tabitha wouldn't let it go. "Come on, talk to me."

Gabriel shifted his weight, causing Tabitha to move.

"I'd rather not be interrogated right now."

"Uh . . . okay. I just thought you might like to talk about it."

Oftentimes they would get close, and Gabriel's mind would go to another place.

Gabriel broke the long, awkward silence. "I think I'm pretty tired." He stood up on the rock.

"We just got here. Are you okay? I wasn't trying to—"

"Yeah, I'm fine." Gabriel interrupted her. His cold demeanor was unexpected.

"You have to let me know what's going on in that head of yours." She tried to soften her tone.

"I don't have to do anything. You coming?"

Tabitha didn't respond. She stood up with him. What started as a flirtatious and intimate moment by the waters turned into an emotional standoff. Gabriel sighed. This had happened before . . . Tabitha pushing her way in, him seeming to shut down. They walked back to the lodge without a word.

"You can take the flashlight." Gabriel handed it to her.

"What's going on?"

"Nothing. I promise. I'm just really tired. I'll talk to you tomorrow." Gabriel turned and disappeared into the woods.

"Good night," she said, but he was already gone.

Gabriel found his way back to the cabin and plopped down on his twin bed. He yanked the chain on his end table lamp to cast light into the musty room. He was angry and didn't know why. He lay on his back, hands clasped across his stomach, one leg dangling off, wondering why he was so restless. He hated the way things had gone with Tabitha. Questions and thoughts played over and over in his mind. After a few self-loathing minutes, he got up, grabbed a flashlight, and headed back outside. He walked along the water's edge for a hundred yards to what the locals called The Reflection Pool. Here it almost seemed as if The River stood still. Other than an occasional river fly or trout flicking the surface of the water, it was like glass. If you sat in the right place on the shore at night, and the moon was bright, you could see a perfect reflecting image of the mountains, trees, and sky. Tabitha said it looked like a Van Gogh.

Gabriel crouched down and leaned over the water. His scruffy beard and curly hair came into focus. A gentle breeze floated through the canyon, tussling the water and blurring his reflection. As the water settled smooth again, he stared into the steel-blue eyes, and it struck him . . . he looked just like his father. The breeze blew again, warmer this time, and it felt like a warm blanket draping over his shoulders. A loud and familiar shriek bounced around the mountain walls. He looked up to see if he could catch a glimpse of the raptor. He had that feeling again, that feeling that he was not alone. As he looked at the image in the water, for a split second, he felt like he heard his father's voice inside him.

I'm so proud of you. You are becoming one with The River.
Was that just me? Dad . . . are you here? Becoming one?

As his internal conversation continued, Gabriel dragged his finger through the reddish clay and formed the symbol that he had seen on the tree and on the cornerstone at the monument.

A chilling wolf cry echoed in the distance. Then a haunting owl hoot seemed to come from right over his shoulder. A few moments later, two river otters scurried across the far side bank before diving into the water and sending ripples across the reflections. It was as if the wildlife were joining the conversation.

His mind flashed to that night on The Beach, nearly a year earlier, when The River stirred, and he experienced what seemed to be a supernatural encounter . . . or dream. He took a seat on the ground facing the pool and the panoramic view of the western skyline. He lay back into the graveled beach and looked up. The expanse of the starlight canopy overhead made him feel small in the canyon.

Gabriel spoke out loud.

"I wish I could talk to you. Can you hear me? I'm sure this is where you'd want me to be, but some days I feel lost. How could I feel at home and lost at the same time?" Gabriel asked, frustrated.

Silence.

Gabriel stared at the night sky.

"What do you want from me, River? I'm here, aren't I?"

More silence.

"I think she wants to fix me. I don't need fixing."

"Who needs fixing?"

Gabriel jumped up and faced the figure walking out of the woods, his heart pounding.

Jacob appeared from the shadows with a grin on his face.

"Who are you talking to out here? It's past midnight."

"What is it with you people and your sneaking up around here?" Gabriel asked, his anger returning.

"I went to get something out of the shed, and I thought I heard something. You good?"

Gabriel sat back down facing the water.

"Yeah," he answered abruptly as he dusted the dirt off of his hands.

Jacob didn't seem to buy it, and he pressed for more. "You sure nothing's bothering you?"

"I'll work it out."

"I'm sorry you had to witness that episode with Billy. There's a lot more to that story."

"Like what?" Gabriel raised a suspect eyebrow as he looked up at Jacob.

"Well, it's a long story. Tomorrow some of the others will get here, and we'll finish up some of our swift-water training. You might want to get some sleep."

"I will."

Jacob turned around and started to walk away. Gabriel, still staring at the water, spoke up again. "I'm just not sure about all this."

Jacob stopped in his tracks and turned around. "What do you mean?"

"All this. Me . . . here at The River. When I first got here, it was amazing, but I just don't know if I'm cut out for this."

Jacob started walking back toward him.

Gabriel continued, "I keep thinking about my mom in Kansas."

"You belong here, Gabriel. You know that," Jacob said confidently.

Gabriel's tone became more indignant. "I do? How do you know? How does anybody know?"

"I just see it in you, like your father."

"Please don't talk about my father, Jacob." Gabriel shook his head.

"Listen, son . . ."

"And don't call me son! I'm the son of John Clarke. You remember, the hero, John Clarke?"

Jacob held up his hands. "Gabriel, I didn't mean to say anything . . . was just—"

Gabriel cut him off. "Right now when I see The River . . . all I see is what could've been . . . what should've been. I see what's gone . . . see who's gone. I guess it's not getting easier. It's getting harder. There were a few days on The River when I felt hopeful. Then we saw those bones . . . that child . . . I don't know, man, something snapped. And I remembered that The River doesn't always give life. Sometimes it takes it."

Jacob sat back down next to Gabriel and let the conversation rest for a few moments before he responded.

"I'm sorry. I'm really sorry. You're still angry with me. I would be too."

Gabriel didn't respond.

"I'll understand if you can't be around me, Gabriel, but Tabitha really loves you."

They both sat in silence, fidgeting with sticks and rocks at the water's edge.

"Do you want to be alone?"

Gabriel nodded.

Jacob stood up and dusted off his jeans. He started to walk away, then paused and looked back.

"Just don't ever let anyone or anything keep you from who you were created to be, Gabriel. People will fail you. I failed you, and I probably will again at some point. But you were created for The River, and no matter what people do or don't do, that will never change. No matter how big the mistake, nobody will ever take that from you. It's who you are. I'm proud of you."

Jacob disappeared back into the forest.

Gabriel considered all that he'd said as he lay back down and drifted off to sleep on the shore of The Reflection Pool.

10

Swift Water Rescue

Sunday Morning—8:30 a.m., On the Deck at The Lodge

A half dozen other guides arrived at Big Water to prepare for the summer season. Most of them had been guiding for a while, but they all were going to get a refresher course of swift-water rescue that day. Jacob was vigilant about training. Many of the guides were ski instructors in the winter and river guides in the summer. No desk jobs for these young people.

The perfect day unfolded with the bright blue sky smiling on the patches of brilliant wildflowers, decorating the landscape around the lodge and the hillside by The River. Blue Flax, Copper Mallows, Wood Lilies, and countless others painted the gray and green terrain. Gabriel, still foggy from falling asleep at The Reflection Pool the night before, lumbered up the steps to join the others. Freddie, Tabitha, and Samuel were sitting at a picnic table on the deck sipping coffee. Freddie cracked a joke and they were doubled over in laughter. Sadie was talking to some of the others who just arrived. Some days it took Gabriel awhile to connect. An introvert by nature, he felt like an outsider, like he was intruding. Everyone was nice enough, but he usually kept to himself around new folks.

"Get your beauty sleep?" Freddie asked Gabriel.

"Hardly."

Gabriel looked at Tabitha. She rose.

"Anyone want some more coffee?" she asked the table.

The guys shook their heads as she turned and headed toward the kitchen.

"Ouch," Samuel commented with a smirk on his face.

"Samuel, is it chilly out here? I think I felt a very cold breeze blow by here." Freddie chuckled at his own sarcasm.

"That was blizzard-like chilly." Samuel turned to Gabriel. "What did you do?"

Gabriel ignored them.

"I better go get some coffee." Gabriel headed toward the kitchen as the door swung open.

"Fresh and hot!"

Ezra shuffled out onto the deck holding a pan of his cinnamon rolls. A hearty cheer erupted. They all swarmed the pan and began tearing off pieces. The icing dripped and the steam rose from the dough. It didn't take long for more reactions to erupt.

"Pure heaven."

"Oh, man . . . this is as good as it gets."

"Ezra, I need to marry a man like you," Sadie said as she took a roll.

"Ezra, can you teach me how to make those?" Freddie didn't waste the opportunity.

"He's relentless," Sadie commented to Ezra.

"You can't blame the kid for tryin'."

Gabriel snatched two rolls and entered the dining area. Tabitha stood behind the counter pouring her coffee.

"Could I get a little of that?"

"Get a mug," she replied shortly.

Gabriel opened the cabinet and pulled out a large white ceramic mug with a yellow daisy painted on it.

She glanced at the mug. "My mom helped me paint that. Be careful with it, please."

"How old were you?"

"Seven." Tabitha stared down at the mug for a moment. "I don't understand you. What was that last night?" she asked, sounding both perturbed and concerned.

Gabriel sighed. "I don't know. I'm not really sure, to be honest."

"Was it something I said? You just shut down. That's not how it works, you know. If you want to have a relationship, you have to relate."

Gabriel was taken aback by her candor. She always spoke her mind so freely.

"You make it sound pretty easy." He passed her the cinnamon roll.

"I didn't say it was easy. Things that are worth it probably aren't easy, right? It takes work."

"I prefer easy."

Tabitha cracked a flirtatious smile as she dipped her finger in the icing.

"You know what's easy?" she asked him.

"What?"

"This!"

Tabitha smeared the icing on Gabriel's nose and ran around the counter and out the door laughing.

"No way."

Gabriel sat in shock for a moment before he hustled out of the kitchen to catch her. He exploded through the door and interrupted Jacob addressing the whole group.

"Welcome, Gabriel," Jacob said sternly.

"Oh, sorry," he answered awkwardly.

Tabitha stood on the other side of the deck grinning from ear to ear. Gabriel caught her eye with a flirtatious glare.

Jacob continued, "Okay guys, let's take as few vehicles as possible, so team up. We're going to do some swift-water exercises at The Carnival. Everyone know where that is?"

The group nodded.

"Yeah, baby!" Freddie shouted as he slammed his hand on the picnic table. "I love that water."

"When we get there, I'll give you more instructions, but we'll do some technical rope rescue exercises, unconscious swimmer extraction, and some good old-fashioned white-water swimming. Freddie, you come with me." Jacob looked up from his clipboard at Freddie.

Freddie gave him a thumbs-up.

Gabriel was still new to the white water. Even though his physique was sculpted and strong, he'd wrestled with debilitating fear his entire life. Anyone would with the things he saw as a young boy. The idea of voluntarily jumping in big water made his stomach jump into his throat. He wanted to back out but wouldn't dare.

———◦◉◦———

The entire Big Water Adventures Team headed down The River in five rafts carrying all the gear necessary for a few hours of training. The morning mist burned off in the canyon as the sun beamed across the water. The temperature was pushed up over eighty degrees.

"I do love this part of The River; it's like a million tiny mirrors sparkling with the sun," Sadie commented with wonder.

"It never gets old, does it?" Gabriel responded.

"Nope."

"How's your leg doing?" he asked as he glanced down.

Sadie turned her knee inward showing her toned calf.

"Just a scar now. Doesn't hurt anymore." She ran her fingers over it.

"Okay, guys, The Carnival is just around the bend, so let's put out in that eddy over there!" Jacob announced as he motioned to all the rafters.

One by one they all pulled in the eddy and beached their rafts.

Jacob's tone turned serious and instructive. "Gather over here and take a seat on these rocks. It's time for a sermon."

The rafters took their seats on the bank of giant boulders facing The River. Jacob continued, "Welcome to The Carnival, ladies and gentlemen. We've got the . . ."

Jacob paused as he noticed Freddie mouthing the words he was saying.

"Freddie, do you have something to say?"

Freddie shook his head violently and put his hand over his mouth.

"You think you know the spiel, wise guy?" Jacob looked serious.

Freddie shook his head again, this time his eyes wide with "uh-oh" written all over them.

Jacob reached in his dry bag and pulled out a folded-up twenty-dollar bill. He held it up so everyone could see it.

"Twenty bucks says you don't know what I'm going to say."

The mood lightened, and then Freddie surprised everyone in a shockingly real "Jacob" voice.

"Welcome to The Carnival, ladies and gentlemen. We've got the best rides in all of Colorado. Most carnivals are fun, but this section of rapids is no joke. I want all eyes on me for the next few minutes as I point out the attractions here at The Carnival. First, you've got the tilt-a-whirl. That's right, it tilts and it whirls . . ."

At this point no one could contain their laughter. Everyone was in stitches, including Jacob.

"Okay, okay!" He waved his hands in surrender.

Jacob waved the twenty-dollar bill in the air and walked over and tucked it in Freddie's lifejacket. Everyone erupted in applause as Freddie took a bow.

"Okay, I'll admit it. That was impressive, Freddie. It's good to have fun. What kind of life do we have, huh? Look around at your office today, guys. Isn't this amazing?" Jacob motioned to the surroundings as he smiled and stroked his salt-and-pepper scruff.

Jacob continued to go over the importance of being vigilant during training. He walked them through all the specific rapids that constituted The Carnival. He went over the dangers of a "haystack" that occurred at the "Ferris wheel" rapid, where the current slowed quickly after a big drop causing a massive standing wave. He warned them of a strainer that had formed down past "pinball." Some dead branches lay across a few rocks allowing the water to pour through, but it was lethal when a person got caught in it. After he finished giving them a verbal tour of the rapids and their challenges, he gave out assignments. Jacob was not only an expert on The River, he was just as strong at imparting his knowledge and explaining the why behind his decisions.

"Okay, guys, we're going to do a little white-water swimming. It's only about three to four feet deep here, so I want us to practice getting into the water off of this rock and then ferrying over to that eddy. Before we do that, I want some upstream and downstream safety in place. Sadie, I want you to head upriver about thirty yards where that tree leans out over the water. Watch for any other boats, logs, or anything that might cause trouble for our swimmers. Samuel, you're one of our strongest swimmers. Why don't you take Jeff with you down to the Ferris wheel in case someone gets past us. He's dead-on with the throw bag. Samuel, take the rope down with you. We'll set up some cross-river lines and do some raft extraction."

Jacob looked at Gabriel.

"You see I spread the team out in areas of their strengths.

This way we have multiple points of rescue instead of all of us being in the same place."

"Got it." Gabriel responded through his nerves as he tightened the straps on his life vest.

Everyone got into position upriver and downriver. Now it was time to practice some swims.

"Freddie, you wanna go first?"

"Sure!" Freddie didn't hesitate. He stepped up on a rock jutting out over the water.

"Freddie!" Jacob yelled.

He turned.

"Your brain bucket?" Jacob pointed to his own head.

"Shoot!" Freddie jumped back down and got his helmet and strapped it on.

Jacob continued instructing. "Okay. Remember, forty-five degree angle to the current. Shallow landing knees; face, feet, and chest hit the water at the same time. Then swim hard."

Freddie didn't waste a second. He got up on the rock and dove without hesitation.

"Go, Freddie!" The others cheered him on.

He smacked the water and immediately started a violent swimming stroke. The water was swift and carried Freddie along as he swam. In a matter of just a few seconds, Freddie traversed the forty feet to the eddy on the other side.

"He's so light and strong he just skips across like a june bug."

Freddie stood up in the eddy and shot everyone a thumbs-up.

"Tabby, you ready?"

"Sure."

Tabitha stepped up and splashed in. Her long, lean body darted across the water in perfect form.

"Wow, she made that look easy," Gabriel commented to Jacob.

A couple more guides followed Tabitha.

"You see how they are doing it? You ready?"

Jacob cinched up the straps on Gabriel's vest. Gabriel tightened his helmet.

"Stay shallow," Jacob said as Gabriel took his position on the rock.

He splashed in. His six-foot-one-inch, one-hundred-eighty-pound frame started the short journey.

"Forty-five!" Gabriel heard Jacob shout. "You're at a ninety. You're going to miss the eddy."

Gabriel pounded the water but could sense his trajectory was already off. He knew the water was not that deep, so he put his feet down to try to wade the final fifteen feet or so.

"Don't stand up! Samuel will get you downriver!" Jacob bellowed, but Gabriel didn't hear him in time. His adrenaline kicked in, and he was reacting. Gabriel looked back as he stood up in the current waist-deep. He glanced forward to see Tabitha and the others telling him to just let go and let the water take him downstream. His instincts wouldn't allow him to surrender to the water, so he plodded one more step.

"No, Gabriel!" Jacob shouted.

The next thing Gabriel knew, his head was bobbing in and out of the water. He gasped for breath every time he hit air, flailing his arms desperately, but he couldn't move.

His foot was stuck under a rock, and he couldn't get enough footing with the other foot to free himself.

Gabriel suddenly saw stars. How long had it been since he'd taken a breath? He tried desperately one last time to free his foot, but the stars were more powerful. He surrendered.

So this is it. The River took my dad, and now it's taking me too.

Suddenly, he was above the water, gasping for air. Jacob was holding on to the back of his life vest.

"Pull yourself up on the rope!" Jacob yelled. Gabriel flailed as Jacob grabbed his wrist and guided his hand to the rope that was positioned directly over his head, with Freddie manning one end on one bank and the other end tied to a tree on the opposite bank. Gabriel mustered the effort to hoist his face up out of the water again. His strength was waning. Then Jacob positioned himself upstream of Gabriel to create an eddy to ease the pressure. He reached down and grabbed Gabriel's foot by the heel and jerked it violently back and forth, and it dislodged.

"Let go!" Gabriel released the rope at Jacob's command, and the two men rode the current feet-first into the next rapid. They cascaded through one hundred yards of white water at the mercy of The River. Jacob held on to Gabriel with his left hand. Samuel cast a throw bag to Jacob and pulled them to safety.

As the two men caught their breath on the shore, Gabriel lay on his back, exhausted. *Jacob saved me. He saved me.* Gabriel unclasped his helmet and looked up at Jacob who was standing over him.

"Thank you," he said faintly.

Jacob removed his vest and helmet.

"That was fun, huh? Let's you know who is in charge out here. That's why they call it the wilderness." Jacob smiled. "I should have reminded you about foot entrapment possibilities. Next time, if you miss your mark, just ride the water feet-first until you can swim out. That's why we have multiple rescue points downstream. Trying to stand up alone in that kind of water can get you killed"—Jacob snapped his fingers—"like that."

The team worked on a few more exercises over the next few hours. Gabriel was embarrassed at the scare he gave everyone. He participated but was distracted at the thought of his close call. He hated everyone asking him if he was okay, especially Tabitha. It made him question things again, feeling like he didn't belong. He wondered if he could really do it. On The River, it felt like there was always something that could go wrong. It was exhilarating and terrifying at the same time. He hated feeling out of control and fearful. He had a long way to go to follow in his father's footsteps.

11

The River Books of Ezra

Monday Night, 9:30 p.m., On the Porch at Ezra's Cabin

The melodic lilting sound and quick tremolo of Ezra's whistling grew louder as Gabriel approached the cabin. He trudged up the steps to see Ezra, rocking back and forth in rhythm. His reading glasses rested halfway down his nose. He sat in a pile of wood shavings as he carved away on a small piece of wood.

"How do you do that?" Gabriel asked.

"Do what?" Ezra looked over his reading glasses at Gabriel without moving his head.

"Whistle, rock, and carve at the same time. I think I'd cut off my finger if I tried that."

Ezra chuckled.

"Maybe they all go together for me or somethin'."

"What are you making?"

"I just started. I'll know soon, though. Sometimes I just have to start, then I get inspired for what the wood wants to reveal."

"So you just start without knowing what you're carving?"

"That's right. If I worry too much about the end at the very beginning, it gets a little too big for my brain to handle. If I just start, then I see where the process takes me. It's fun to be surprised and trust the wood and the knife."

"I'm going to grab a quick shower. It's been a long day. Maybe I'll join you when I'm done."

"I would like that."

Gabriel knew deep down that he was supposed to be at The River. Parts of him were coming alive to the exhilaration of adventure in this new life. He was learning more every day about what it meant to be a guide. Jacob told him about how you learn just by running The River. The challenges that arise teach you. The guides who have gone before teach you. You can only learn so much from the shore, and then you just have to ride the waves. His love for Tabitha grew by the day, but learning to relate to her was brand new. He certainly didn't want to go back to the five-and-dime in Cairo, but embracing this newfound world felt risky. Life at The River was pregnant with the possibility for incredible life-changing experiences, both good and bad. His childhood fears of water and death were real, and they gripped his mind from time to time. With each passing day, he felt like he moved further away from those painful memories that tried to control him, and that was good.

———◆———

"You done yet?" Gabriel said sarcastically as he let the flimsy screen door to his room slam.

Ezra held up the pineapple-sized chunk of wood. A couple of divots that loosely resembled eyes were emerging.

"Well, it's got eyes, I see." Gabriel squinted and tilted his head as he looked.

"I believe I know who this is going to be now. She's beautiful." Ezra stared at the lump of wood.

Gabriel sat down, his bushy blond hair only towel-dried. He breathed in deeply and rested his head on the back of the wooden rocker. The air was damp and cool. The sound of The River moving just a few yards away created a lush and unceasing ambience.

"Why is it hard to talk about things, Ezra?" Gabriel stared ahead.

"What things?"

"I don't know. I just find it hard to . . ."

"Let people in?" Ezra finished his sentence.

"Yeah, I guess."

"Half the battle is admitting it isn't easy for you. Things take time."

"I see some of the others, and it's easy for them. Like Tabitha . . . she's uninhibited."

Ezra kept carving.

"Maybe I just overthink things."

Ezra looked over the top of his reading glasses at Gabriel.

"Thinking is not a bad thing. That's why the Maker gave

you a brain. The trick is thinking right and true . . . especially about you."

"What do you mean by that?"

Ezra paused.

"What are you afraid of?"

"Huh?"

"What are you afraid of?" Ezra asked again.

"I don't know . . . Losing someone I care about, maybe."

"That all?"

"The white water can be pretty scary."

"Oh, yes, it can."

Gabriel wondered where this was going.

"What about you, Ezra?"

"What about me?"

"What are you afraid of?"

"Too many things to count . . . have been my whole life."

Gabriel was surprised by Ezra's answer.

"Really? You always seem so calm, not fazed by anything."

"Fear comes to us all. Anyone who says they aren't afraid of anything is saying that straight through their terrified teeth." Ezra chuckled. "For starters, they are afraid of what people would think of them if they knew they were scared. Everyone has fear. Ah, but courage in the face of fear, now that's the good stuff."

"How did you come to The River, Ezra?"

"Oh, that's a long story."

"I'm in no hurry."

Ezra held up the piece he was working on.

"Look at that."

He showed it to Gabriel.

"What?"

"Look right there. The wood had a crack on the inside. How about that? I cut that piece out and there it was. Now that line will go right down her cheek. Interesting."

It was just past ten thirty, and large raindrops, one at a time, began to pelt the tin roof of the old cabin. *Splat. Splat. Split splat.* They sped up into a steady downpour.

"I love that sound," Gabriel commented as he looked out and saw the rain droplets shimmer in the porch light. "It reminds me of the sound of rain on the barn back in Cairo. I would go out there and sit on Mr. Earl's tractor, especially on hard days. Sometimes I just cried and cried, and when the rain came, it felt like maybe God knew how sad I was. The rain made me feel like He was crying with me. Sounds silly saying it out loud."

"That's not silly at all. Don't discount those things you feel. When it feels like the Maker is crying with you, I think He probably is."

"So you believe in God?"

"From the top of my head all the way down to the bottom of my shoes."

"I want to. There's just too much suffering. I don't know how a God . . . at least a good God, could allow that." Ezra didn't respond. Gabriel leaned back in his chair to ponder his statement before he continued. "I'm still waiting on an answer to my first question."

The rain slowed to a soft and steady shower.

"What question, son? You remember I'm old."

"How did you come to The River?"

Ezra set his carving down and grabbed his antique pipe

and tobacco tin off of the old wood barrel they used as a table. His thick, weathered hands packed a pinch into the pipe bowl.

"It was bad . . . real bad . . . if you looked like this." Ezra rubbed the dark-brown wrinkled skin of his right hand with his left.

"My momma worked for a very wealthy family in Mississippi. She cleaned their house, cooked dinners, and did all sorts of chores for them. They had a large cotton farm, a few cattle, and some chickens. We lived in a tiny room off the back of the house. It wasn't much, but it was somethin'."

Ezra struck a match on the barrel and lit the pipe. After several rapid tokes, he shook the match out and laid it on the barrel. The nutty vanilla smoke floated across the porch and into the rain.

"I tried to be the man of our little house, since I had no daddy around. My momma never said too much about him; she would just kiss my forehead and say, 'God will get us through.' I never knew Him. Oh, did I hate going to school. The stuff the kids would say was just awful. The names and the insults never stopped. I remember one day in grade school it was a scorcher. I was so thirsty I just took a drink out of the first drinking fountain I came to. Wham! I felt a smack on the back of my head, jammed my mouth into the spicket. My lip was bleeding somethin' fierce. I turned around to see an older white boy pointing to the sign above the fountain. 'Can't you read, nig—?' I don't even want to say it." Ezra started to smile. "He didn't even know what he was doin'. Just the product of an angry home."

Gabriel hung on every word in a concentrated stare.

"One day, I was about sixteen years old or so, when I came back from fishing in a small pond on the back of the property. I used to catch some good catfish in there."

Gabriel interrupted, "That's where the legend of Ezra's fishing started, then, huh?"

The old man smiled as he continued.

"It was a beautiful late afternoon. Sun was going down. I still remember how the dandelions exploded into the air as I kicked my old boots through the field. I came around the edge of the old barn carrying a string of two- and three-pounders over my shoulder. As I looked up . . . the site I saw still haunts me to this day." Ezra took a deep breath and looked away. "I need some hot cocoa. You want some?" His husky voice quivered. Ezra stood up abruptly and went into his room.

"Sure," Gabriel answered through the screen door.

He leaned back in his rocker and wondered what the next part of the story held.

Ezra emerged a few minutes later with two mugs. He handed Gabriel one and lowered himself gingerly into his rocker.

"Ezra, if you don't want to talk about it . . ."

"It's okay."

He sipped from the steaming mug.

"That man had his back to me. Then I heard him shout, 'How dare you steal from me after all I've done for you!' I could tell he'd been drinkin'. He would get powerful mean on the bottle. My momma was on her knees looking up at him like a beggar. She was cryin'. She said, 'I didn't take nothin'!' He wasn't having any of it. He balled his fist and hit my momma so hard I thought her head would come off. I was so angry. Momma was out cold on the ground, and then he started to kick her. I threw my pole and the fish down and started runnin'."

Ezra paused, sniffed, and gathered his composure before he continued.

"I think he would've killed her. I saw a rock the size of that carving down there. I picked it up and . . . Mistah Jones never kicked or insulted my momma again."

Gabriel didn't speak.

"I ain't proud of what I did. I didn't want him to die. I just wanted him to stop."

After several seconds of waiting, Gabriel broke the silence. "Ezra, I had no idea."

"I haven't told that to too many people, son."

"Did your mom recover?"

"I was in the hospital with Momma that night, and the police came and took me away. They took me out back and gave me a beating I'll never forget. I thought I'd never get out of that cell. She came and saw me in prison every Sunday . . . Yep, she never missed. She got real sick and passed away while I was in there. I still remember the Sunday she didn't show up. Mrs. Jones, the widow of the man I killed, did. She gave me a letter from Momma and said some words to me that I carry with me to this day."

Ezra sat up in his chair and looked over into Gabriel's eyes.

"She said, 'Ezra, you are a good boy. Mr. Jones . . . he wasn't right in his mind, and what he did to your momma was pure evil. I'm working on some things for you. I'm trying to get you out of here. You deserve a new beginning.'

With that she just walked out and I never saw her again. The next day they came and got me. The officers told me the judge said I was free to go. Just like that. So there I was, a twenty-three-year-old orphaned black man, free as a bird, with nowhere to go and not a dime to my name."

He tipped his mug all the way up to get the last bit of chocolate out.

"I think this is a two-cup story, Gabriel. You want some more?"

The old man inched his way to the edge of the rocker and got up again.

"Okay, sure. But I have to hear more, if you're up to it."

While Ezra disappeared back into his room to make another cup, Gabriel sat ruminating on all that he just heard. The suffering, the injustice, the fact that Ezra grew up in the back of a farmhouse without a father . . . it was surreal . . . almost too much to take in.

Ezra emerged with two more steaming cocoas.

"Now we're gettin' to the good part."

"I'm ready," Gabriel said as he took the mug from Ezra.

"I went through a pretty bad spell there for a while. I couldn't get anyone to hire me. So I took some things from people. Money when I could. I got into people's gardens and got fresh raw vegetables. I even stole a bicycle and just started ridin'. I didn't even know where I was goin'. I made my way right out of Mississippi, up through Arkansas, and I even went through Kansas."

"No way! Did you go through Cairo?"

"I think I got close." Ezra flashed his contagious grin.

"This is unbelievable." Gabriel shook his head.

"I was homeless and on the run. I was at a filling station when this old pickup truck pulled in. I saw this man get out and walk to pay for his gas. I snuck around and took a look in his truck to see if I could find somethin' I could use. And then I heard that voice. 'Hey, son! Son! What are you doin?'"

"This man came walking up to me. I don't know what happened but I couldn't run. I just froze. I backed up against his truck. He approached me with kindness in his eyes.

"'You need something? You hungry? I got a sandwich in there that's yours if you want it.'"

Ezra's voice began to quiver.

"Who does that? Who offers a man a sandwich when he darn well knew I was gonna steal from him? Then he asked me my name. I told him. He said, 'That's a good name, son.' He asked me if I knew what my name meant. I said, 'No, sir.' He told me Ezra means 'help.' He gave me the best ham sandwich I'd ever had that day. He asked me if I wanted a job and I said, 'Yes, sir!' That man brought me to The River. I've never left. That man . . . was R. Allen Clarke . . . your grandfather."

Gabriel felt this to his core. A sense of honor toward his ancestor washed over him as Ezra continued.

"When I came to work for the Clarkes all those years ago, I was low. I didn't know which way was up. I asked your grandpa if I could get a piece of bread after I was done cleaning up the yard, 'cause I was so hungry. I remember Mister Clarke's huge hand wrapping around my shoulder. He walked me into the house. I thought I was in big trouble. He was a big man. I can still hear his voice. 'You see this house? This is your house.' Then he walked me into the back bedroom where he had me stayin'. 'You see this bed? This is your bed.' Then he walked me into the kitchen and opened the icebox."

Ezra's voice started to break up. "He opened it up and said, 'You see this food? It's your food. You are one of us now. You are a son of this house. What's ours is yours. You don't ever have to ask.'"

Ezra looked away and wiped his eyes. "That day changed my life. I could get in the pantry myself? No one ever treated me like that." Ezra smiled and wagged his finger as he reminisced. "That . . . that is love . . . and when love comes . . . freedom comes too. Yes, sir. Love found me. Real love. I know who I am and where I belong. We need more people like your grandfather in this world. People who will reach down and lift someone up . . . treat them like they are worth something . . . believe in them. That kind of greatness . . . that's what you come from, son. You see, your grandfather reminded me I had a purpose and that I was worthy. You, Gabriel, are worthy."

12

Under the Waterfall

Later that Summer—July 28, 1973

Gabriel's first full summer at The River was one of discovery, connection, and new beginnings. He was a long way from his frightened and tumultuous childhood in Cairo, Kansas. As a twenty-one-year-old, new horizons were in view. His perspective on life was changing. He began to see life as it could be, not as it was. Little by little and moment by moment, The River was invigorating Gabriel's soul. Places in his heart that were numb with shame, fear, and grief were coming alive again. Places in his soul that were heavy with anger and resentment for what he'd lost were giving way to days full of wonder and gratitude.

He was getting his footing as a guide now. He moved

from assisting and prepping runs to actually guiding a few of his own trips down on Class II and III rapids. He fell in love with helping people experience the grandeur and beauty of The River. Serving others got him out of his own head and brought him unceasing passion. The more people he helped, the more excitement he felt.

After another mouthwatering breakfast with the others on the deck of the lodge, Gabriel went down to the gear shed to find out his assignment for the day. Jacob was already there, writing names on the large chalkboard behind the counter. His day got exponentially better when he saw whom he was guiding with.

Gabriel (Lead)/Tabitha (Asst)
Half-Day Family
Stevenson (4)

Gabriel felt a soft and cool hand slip inside his left bicep as he was looking at the board.

"So I guess I'm with you today. You okay with that, mister?" Tabitha grabbed his arm with both hands and pulled him close.

"Yes, ma'am. I'm very good with that. As long as you behave yourself and don't give me any trouble." He matched her flirtatious tone.

"What makes you think I'd give you any trouble?"

"Well, that's your middle name, isn't it . . . Trouble?"

"Excuse me?" she said as she raised her eyebrows and walked over to the life vest racks.

Gabriel couldn't help but let his eyes wander, watching her curves as she moved across the room. She looked amazing to Gabriel, no matter what she wore.

"Gabriel," Jacob said sternly as he peered over his reading glasses.

"Yes, sir?" Gabriel, embarrassed, turned his head to Jacob so fast he almost gave himself whiplash.

"Why is your face turning so red, son?"

"Uh, not sure." Gabriel rubbed his neck. "I'll go get the rig ready."

"Good idea," Jacob said without a smile.

It was nine thirty a.m., and the two Jeeps were prepped and ready to head out for the family float trip. One hauled the trailer with the raft, all the gear, paddles, the cooler, and the life vests. The other Jeep would carry the rafters to the put-in.

The young family arrived at the gear shed after checking in, and Tabitha greeted them.

"Hi, guys! I'm Tabitha. I'll be one of your guides today. Is this your first time?"

The family of four all nodded with nervous excitement.

The dad held out his hand. "I'm Brian, this is my wife, Kim, and this is our daughter, Samantha . . . She's ten, and our son, Johnny. He's five."

The towheaded little boy hid behind his father's leg.

Brian ruffled Johnny's hair. "He's a little nervous."

Gabriel walked up and joined the interchange.

"How are you guys doing? You ready for some white water today?"

"Yes, we are." The mild-mannered father looked down

at his son who was clutching his leg even tighter. "It's going to be fun. You don't have anything to be afraid of."

Gabriel got down on one knee. "What's your name, little man?"

The boy just buried his head in his dad's leg.

"Johnny. Yep, this one is scared of his own shadow. We thought this might be good for him," Brian said as he stroked his son's head.

Gabriel looked up at the dad. "Where are you guys from?"

"Witchita."

"Really? I lived in Kansas for fifteen years! You *must* be awesome if you live in Kansas." Gabriel directed his comment to the boy.

The kindergartner cracked a smile as he peeked around his dad's leg.

"There it is. I knew you were a river guy."

Gabriel worked hard to put the entire family at ease. On the forty-five-minute drive up to the put-in, he found out that Brian, a small-framed man with blond hair and wire-frame glasses, was an accountant. He was quite measured and quiet in his communication. His wife, Kim, a perky and round five-foot-tall brunette, was a high school art teacher. She wasn't short on words. They were on their first vacation out west.

They pulled the Jeeps off the paved road onto the well-worn clearing next to The River.

"Okay, guys. Just meet me over on that rock, and we'll go over some safety stuff."

They climbed out and headed that way. At ten o'clock,

the eighty-five degree dry air made for a perfect day to be on the water.

While Tabitha helped everyone get their life vests fastened properly, Gabriel single-handedly dragged the fourteen-foot raft off the trailer and into the water. He went over the basics of his safety talk, and then little Johnny started to whimper.

"I don't want to go. I don't want to go."

"You sure, buddy? We might see some really beautiful wildlife out there today! Maybe even an otter or two." Gabriel tried to reach out to the boy.

"It's going to be fun," Brian responded.

Johnny ran to his mom and jumped into her arms.

"I wanna go home!"

Gabriel looked at the mom and dad. "It's okay. There's no rush." He held his finger up as an idea came to him. "I'll be right back." Gabriel ran up to the Jeep and came back in less than a minute. "Hey, Johnny, come here, buddy. Have you ever seen one of these?"

Kim put the little boy down and he walked over to Gabriel who was crouched down. As Johnny approached the guide, he held up a large silver, blue, and gray Aggie marble.

"It's a magic river marble."

Johnny looked back at his mom and dad, and his countenance immediately lifted.

"Wow!" Kim said, playing along.

Gabriel held it up to the sunlight and pointed to it.

"You see those beautiful lines in there? That's The River running inside the marble. If you hold on to this marble, it will chase away the fear so you can ride the water. Would you like to have it?"

The wide-eyed boy nodded his head enthusiastically.

"Awesome. Now, don't lose it. In fact, you can also spend some time steering the raft with me if you keep it with you. Would you like that?"

"Can I make it go fast?"

"Absolutely!"

The parents cheered with relief. Gabriel noticed how intently Tabitha watched him, and he gave her a wink.

"Hey, Johnny, come over here for a second."

He motioned for the boy to join him at the water's edge.

"If you put the marble in the water before we get in, you'll see how it shines and looks even more beautiful."

Johnny lowered his chubby hand, holding the marble into the shallow water.

"You see? Everything shines more beautifully in The River, Johnny."

The boy stared at his marble, lost in wonder.

Johnny got in the raft after that without hesitation. Gabriel pushed off the shore and jumped on the back tube. Johnny immediately crawled to sit with him.

Gabriel grabbed his vest and pulled him in right beside him.

"You ready?"

Johnny nodded.

"You got your marble?"

"Yep!" The rosy-cheeked little guy held it up in the sunlight as he squinted his bright blue eyes.

The young family and the two guides had a glorious few hours on The River, complete with small cascading rapids, a nice picnic, and a splash fight to end their time together.

As they were getting the gear out of the raft and preparing to make the ride back to camp, Kim took Gabriel and Tabitha aside.

"I can't thank you enough for an amazing trip today. You don't know how much it meant to us that you helped Johnny overcome his fear. I wasn't sure we were going to be able to make the trip, but you saved it for him . . . and us. The experience was more than we could have hoped for."

"He's an awesome kid. We had a blast with you today. I hope you'll come back," Gabriel said with a comforting smile.

"Oh, we will. By the way, how did you know he loves marbles so much? He has a whole collection of them at home!"

"I didn't. But, hey, what kid doesn't love marbles, right?" Gabriel looked at Tabitha as Kim walked away.

"Are you kidding me? What are the chances of that?" he asked quietly.

Tabitha shook her head in amazement.

Sadie and Freddie brought the Jeeps to the load-out area and drove everyone home. They arrived back at the lodge around four p.m. and said their good-byes to the tourists from Wichita.

As Gabriel was hanging the life vests up to dry, Tabitha grabbed his hand and pulled. She walked backward, leading him out of the gear shed as she spoke.

"I made some fresh coffee, and I have some of those chocolate chip cookies you like. Go get cleaned up and meet me at the Jeep in twenty minutes. I want to take you somewhere."

"Yes, ma'am," Gabriel said with a wondering smile and raised eyebrows.

He had never had a real girlfriend before Tabitha. Every step, every encounter was new and wonderful. Even when it was hard, he was grateful for the companionship.

Gabriel approached the Jeep. Tabitha sat in the driver's seat, revving the engine, ready to put it into gear.

"Come on, slowpoke." She smiled as she pulled her long hair back into a ponytail.

Gabriel grabbed the roll bar and hoisted himself in the passenger side.

"Where're we going, Miss Fielding?"

"You'll see."

They headed northwest on the highway for about thirty minutes, climbing higher into the gorge as the road switched back and forth. The old Jeep chugged as they pulled off the road. Tabitha grabbed her backpack out of the back and threw it on her shoulders.

"This way," she said as she took his hand and led him into the forest. As they trekked deeper in the canyon woods, the thunderous roar of the water grew louder.

"Not too many people even know about this spot. It's one of my favorites."

They exited the trees onto the edge of a cliff that overlooked a spectacular waterfall cascading down some fifty feet or more.

"The River divides around this mountain; half flows down these falls and half flows on the other side, meeting up down there," Tabitha explained. "Be careful. The rocks are slick from the mist."

The young couple hugged a narrow path on the canyon wall that descended down about twenty feet. The path curved back into a large cave and opened up right underneath the powerful cascade. The mist sprayed into the air off the jagged rocks on either side. The unceasing flow created a beautiful haven underneath the mountain.

Tabitha removed a colorfully striped wool blanket from her backpack and spread it on the cool moss-covered rock.

Gabriel stood close to the edge, experiencing the power of the water as it flowed over their heads.

"I never tire of the sound of water. It just speaks to me."

His voice echoed against the rock cave.

Tabitha sat down on the blanket. Gabriel turned around and sat next to her. It suddenly occurred to him how alone and secluded they were. It was magical.

"This is one of my favorite spots in the entire canyon. I feel safe here. It's such a refuge." Tabitha leaned her head on Gabriel's shoulder. His heart thumped.

"The River keeps surprising me. Just when I think I've seen it all, there's more, and it keeps getting more interesting and beautiful."

Tabitha picked her head up and leaned in to kiss Gabriel.

She pulled her head back and stared into his eyes.

They kissed again.

She smiled.

"You taste like chocolate." Then it dawned on her. "Did you steal a cookie?"

Gabriel shrugged his shoulders as he grinned.

She smudged the lip gloss from his lips with her thumb.

"You are so guilty."

She backed up and grabbed her thermos and pulled two mugs out of her backpack.

"I'm warning you; this is my sweet coffee, not that motor oil you boys drink."

"I'm sure I'll love it," he said as she poured them a couple of cups.

They sat facing each other with their legs crossed.

"Here's to little Johnny and that sweet family." She held her mug up and Gabriel joined her as they toasted the beautiful moment. "I'm still in awe of how you helped that little boy. You have a way with kids, I guess. It made my heart melt . . . even more. And to us . . . you and me . . ." They tapped their mugs again.

After a few seconds of quiet and another brief kiss, she spoke up.

"What do you think about us, Gabriel?" she asked tenderly.

"What do I think?" he repeated as he thought about a response.

"Yeah, what do you think about us? About me? I know that you have feelings for me, but you don't really say much. I've just been wondering where this is going . . . what's going on in that heart of yours," she said as she traced her finger along the edge of the blanket.

Gabriel felt the longing in her voice. It hit him like the power of the water pouring in front of them. He had never told her how he really felt. He never really knew how to express what was in his heart. It just seemed too risky. It was all so new. He didn't want to mess anything up.

Gabriel paused in thought as he looked away.

Tabitha sighed. "If you're not ready to talk about this, it's okay. I guess . . ."

"I love you," he blurted out. His eyes became moist and red as he continued nervously.

"I love you. More than anything or anyone, I think. Since the first time I laid eyes on you, it's like my heart has been outside of my chest. I don't know exactly what's next . . . I don't. I do know this. No one has ever made me feel more alive than you. I'm just better with you." Tabitha sat speechless as he continued. "Your beauty . . . it keeps me awake at night. My words get tangled when you come into the room. You've got me inside out, Tabitha Fielding."

Tabitha cupped her hand over her mouth as a tear melted down her cheek. She wrapped her arms around his neck and hugged him fiercely. He could feel tears on his neck.

"I love you, Gabriel Clarke. I love you."

13

Anniversary

After that day under the waterfall with Tabitha, Gabriel felt like his feet didn't touch the ground for days. To have this kind of love for a woman, and to have her love him back, was more than he ever dreamed. When they weren't guiding a raft together, they took long walks along The River, went swimming at the cliffs with friends, or they would sit under the stars and Gabriel would read to her from The Journal.

Gabriel's first summer becoming a guide in Colorado brought The River to the very center of who he was. His calling became clearer. His confidence as a guide grew with every trip. He felt like he was becoming who he was meant to be.

On a warm morning in early August, before his day of guiding began, Gabriel sat, legs dangling on the edge of the porch. With Rio's head resting on his thigh, he read an entry in The Journal. The words sank into his heart as he stroked the head of the old husky.

> Sadness falls like a heavy blanket. Sometimes it smothers me. Why must the hard times come? At times I get over-whelmed. But it is in those times that I feel The River closest. It's in the pain, the longing, and the grief that I somehow know there *IS* joy and hope. How? My soul opens up at the deepest levels when the suffering comes. And when my soul opens up . . . and the joy comes . . . and it does come . . . I feel it deeper and more abiding. I see beauty more radiant, and my connections with those closest to me go deeper still. The sadness may last through the night, but my joy will return with the sun-rise. Life comes out of death.

After another rewarding day of guiding on the water, Gabriel headed out of the gear shed toward the path to his cabin to get a shower. Tabitha called out to him from behind the counter.

"Remember tonight! Don't forget your stone and your card!" she exclaimed in a hushed voice.

Gabriel gave her the okay sign as he walked into the woods. He approached the cabin to see Ezra whittling away on his woodcarving. Rio slept quietly on his side next to Gabriel's rocking chair.

"How's your day been, Ezra?"

"F-a-n-tastic."

"Good to hear. I'm beat. I had two great runs on the water today. No swimmers and the water was high. Good times." Gabriel turned his attention to his dog.

"Rough day at the office for you too?" He tussled the loose fur on the back of the dog's neck. Rio opened his eyes slowly and then closed them again.

"That dog has the life . . . horizontal all day."

"That's not like him. Hmm. I'll see you over at dinner. I'm going to grab a shower," Gabriel said as he kicked off his sandals next to his screen door.

"I'm actually going to stay here and work on this piece for a while. Jacob told me he had dinner covered. You kids have a good time."

Gabriel poked his head back out of the screen door. "Can I bring you something from the kitchen?"

"No, thank you, son. I'll be just fine."

The entire Big Water Adventures Team assembled out on the deck at the lodge for dinner. The smoky smell from the burgers smoldering over a hickory wood fire made Gabriel's mouth water.

Freddie manned the large outdoor grill with great enthusiasm.

"Grab your buns, people! Hold 'em tight! I've got burgers comin' off this grill that are going to change your life tonight!"

His lisped poem rallied everyone to grab a hamburger roll amidst the laughter.

Freddie placed a burger on each roll as the guides passed through the line like soldiers in a mess hall. The drinks were stacked in large tin washbasins filled with ice. Bags of potato chips, condiments, and jars of pickles were spread around the picnic tables. Stories from The River filled the starlit evening.

Jacob came up the steps to the deck and whistled to get everyone's attention.

"The bonfire is going at The Reflection Pool, guys. Everything is set up. Don't forget a chair or blanket if you want something to sit on. Gabriel, you and Tabitha are responsible for getting Ezra there. Sadie, don't forget your ukulele. Remember, everyone, bring your card and be ready with your 'thank you stone.' We will put them all in the box and present it to him, okay? This is going to be awesome. This man has meant so much to all of us. It's going to be a special night. Let's meet down there in about fifteen minutes."

The group finished up their meals, cleaned up the deck, and headed down to the bonfire. Gabriel and Tabitha made their way to the cabin.

When they got close, Gabriel called, "Ezra! Ezra! Could you come with us for a minute? We found something down at The Reflection Pool that you need to see."

"My goodness. What's all the fuss?" Ezra asked through his pipe-holding clinched teeth as he focused on his carving.

Gabriel grinned at Tabitha. "It won't take long, but you aren't going to believe what we found!"

Ezra peered up from his rocker. "What is it?"

"We can't explain it; you just have to see it!"

"All right. Let me get my sweater." He set his carving down, retrieved his thick cardigan sweater from inside, and followed them on the path by the banks.

"We thought you might know what this is," Gabriel said over his shoulder as he led the way with a flashlight.

Ezra watched his feet to keep from stumbling, Tabitha holding his arm, as they emerged from the trees into the clearing next to the water.

Before he looked up, Sadie started strumming the ukulele in a mountain rhythm and all twenty-two Big Water Team members stood in a half circle behind the roaring fire clapping in rhythm on the upbeat.

The sound startled Ezra. He looked up and saw them, smiling faces lit with a flickering orange glow from the flames. Gabriel and Tabitha walked over and joined the team and they all sang.

"Wade out in the water! Wade out in the w-a-t-e-r!"

Ezra began to laugh and lifted his hands in the air.

"What is this?"

They all kept singing, and the old man walked over and started slapping his thigh and singing with them. Gabriel could feel the joy like electricity.

As the chorus came to a natural ending, they all applauded and whistled for several seconds.

"We love you, Ezra!" they shouted.

He stared with his mouth open.

"I love you too! What in the world is goin' on here?"

Jacob laughed as he walked over and put his arm around the much shorter man.

"Ezra, several years ago you told me the date that you

arrived at The River. You told me how it changed every-thing for you, and you would never forget that date. I wrote it down and didn't want to forget it. Well, Ezra, I know this is probably not news to you, but today marks your fiftieth anniversary of coming to The River." The group erupted again in cheers and applause.

"You have been cooking for us, guiding us, serving us, and, most of all, loving us, and we want to tell you that we honor you and we are so thankful for you. Our words fall short, and I know my words cannot come close to express-ing how much you mean to us."

Jacob took a deep breath before he continued.

"You help us see life through The River's lens, Ezra. I would not be here without you. This operation would not be what it is without you. So happy fiftieth!"

The cheers erupted again.

"I don't know what to say." Ezra looked at the ground shaking his head. "I got no words."

"Well, you don't have to say anything right now. Just enjoy the fact that all these people here think the world of you. We've got hot cocoa going, and melted chocolate to dip your roasted marshmallows, so enjoy!"

Many of the guides came over to hug Ezra. They all milled around, roasting their marshmallows and sharing stories by the firelight. As they settled into the chairs and blankets around the fire, Jacob got everyone's attention again.

"Ezra, I'm going to need you to take a seat over here."

Freddie came walking out of the woods with Ezra's rocking chair and placed it at the north end of the fire.

Jacob continued, "Ezra, I made this box for you."

The lead guide held up a beautiful hand-hewn wooden box.

"Several years ago I was able to get this reclaimed wood from the porch of the original Clarke home in Corley Falls, where you first lived at The River. I've saved it for this special day." He lifted the lid on the box and showed it to Ezra. "Inside there are cards from all of us to you." He closed the lid back down. "You'll see on the top, all of our initials are carved around the edges, and in the center, the symbol of Ama-Woya."

Ezra's eyes welled and his scruffy lip quivered as he ran his hands over the carved initials. Tabitha squeezed Gabriel's hand.

"History," Ezra whispered softly.

"Ezra, we each have a small river stone; they are 'thank you stones,' really. On one side, we painted our initials and on the other a word to represent what you mean to us. Each of us will bring the stones and put them in the box, and as we do, we are going to tell you what the word is and why. I'll begin." Jacob took a small, smooth stone out of his pocket. "I wrote the word *wisdom*, Ezra. You have guided me for the better part of two decades. There are so many words really. But I want you to know, I couldn't imagine where I'd be without your wisdom."

One by one, the team filed by Ezra's rocker to place their stones in the box.

Kind

Gentle

Friend

Humble

Forgiving

Strong

Ezra looked each one in the eye as they spoke. He embraced their hands as they dropped the stones in the box. Tabitha and Gabriel went last.

"Ezra, I wanted to write a thousand words. To choose one was just excruciating." Tabitha chuckled through her tears and wiped her eyes. "I chose *generous*. You give yourself away in countless ways every day. Your smile, a kind word, a cinnamon roll, a piece of advice, a hug . . . You're a gift to all of us Ezra, and I love you." Tabitha leaned down and embraced him for several seconds.

"Thank you, princess," he muttered.

Gabriel stepped up to Ezra and looked at the group. He took a deep breath and glanced up to the stars.

"Oh, man, I'm not sure I can get through this. Give me a minute." He paused . . . another deep breath. "Ezra, I came to The River a broken and devastated man. I've got so much further to go, but you never judged me. You kept me close and helped me down the road of becoming. I'm forever indebted to you." Gabriel wiped his eyes on his sleeve as he held up his stone. "I chose the word *champion* . . . I think my dad would have too. You have been in my corner, helping me, cheering me on, never letting me lose sight of myself or The River along the way. You always have the right words to say. I don't know how you do that." Gabriel heard chuckles of agreement. "Thank you for being my champion, Ezra."

Gabriel placed the last stone in the box and bent down to hug his mentor.

"Happy fifty years, Ezra!" Jacob shouted.

The singing started again as they celebrated into the night, the man who had helped so many.

The next morning, Gabriel woke at daybreak, still basking in the glow of the celebration the night before. In his sweatpants and undershirt, he stepped out onto the porch to check the temperature, but something was missing. It was Rio. The canine never failed to jump up and greet his master when he heard the screen door. Not today. Gabriel slipped on his boots and went down the steps. He began whistling softly and called out just above a whisper, "Rio. Rio. Here, boy!"

No answer.

Gabriel walked to the water's edge and looked upstream. He called a little louder this time. "Rio! Rio! It's time for breakfast! Here, boy!"

No answer. Could he have tangled with a bear? Surely Gabriel would have heard that.

Gabriel turned downstream and walked a little farther. The magpies and swallows accompanied the soft-flowing waters with their chirping. The sun broke over the mountain, and its rays beamed through the mist of the morning fog. The heavenly morning walk gave way to a sight that made Gabriel's heart sink. There, just a few yards downstream, was his beloved furry companion of nearly ten years, lying quiet with his ice-blue eyes closed, his head resting on a rock. The water gently lapped the tip of his tail. Gabriel ran to him and collapsed at his side in the wet dirt.

"Rio! Hey, boy, it's me."

No response.

Gabriel laid his head down on the dog's rib cage, trying

to detect a heartbeat or sounds of breath, but to no avail. He sat up and held Rio's lifeless paw.

"Did you leave me, Rio? You can't leave me. It's just starting to get good, boy. I didn't know you were sick." Gabriel stroked his fur as he looked around the canyon. "You gotta come back, Rio. Come on. You saved my life!"

Alone in the quiet of the morning, draped across his beloved Rio, Gabriel wept. The faithful friend who gave him courage and comfort during the darkest times of his life was gone.

———◆———

There wasn't a dry eye in the semicircle of guides as Gabriel poured the last bit of dirt out of the shovel onto the wooden box that held his fiercest protector and most loyal companion. The River cascaded in the background as they stood in silence around the freshly turned dirt that late morning at the Cathedral of the Sun. Gabriel jammed the shovel in the dirt and relived memories with the group as he stared at the grave.

"He actually saved my life. That's how I met him. I would have stepped right on that snake, and here comes this wolf charging . . . I thought he was going to attack me and . . . he dove into the dirt and bit the head right off that rattler! Yeah, he picked me. He never left my side after that. He listened to me many a night when I didn't know what to do. Sometimes the best of friends don't have all the answers. They are just there . . . with you."

The others took bunches of wildflowers they'd picked and one by one rested them on the mound of dirt.

"I'm so sorry, bud." Jacob put his hand on Gabriel's shoulder.

Sadie's lilting vocal filled the canyon air.

If your heart is heavy on the lonesome road, wade out in
the water,
If the burden from your journey's got you way down low,
wade out in the water.
Oh the sun is shining on the other shore, wade out in the
water.
'Cause saddened hearts and cryin' eyes will be no more,
wade out in the water.
Wade out in the water. Wade out in the water.

Gabriel felt like one of heaven's angels was singing in nature's cathedral that day. The grief was real and heavy, but the load was shared in the loving arms of friends.

14

The Letters

October 4, 2012, 6:30 a.m.

With every labored step, my lungs burned with the morning air. The steam from each exhale clouded my eyes. The changes in elevation really took me off guard. The steep grades and the altitude shortened my normal five miles to about three. Running has always been my release. It's where I think and process life. Running in the mountains, in the wilderness, was a different experience. I felt like I was in a movie. Toward the end of my run that morning, it did occur to me that these woods were teeming with wildlife far more powerful and fast than I. That helped me pick up the pace. Imagining a grizzly bear in pursuit of me in the morning twilight improved my ability to push through the pain on the last half mile.

During the run, I couldn't stop thinking about Gabriel's

story. It was so surreal, these people, these experiences. To see someone who had experienced such tragedy and suffering and still find beauty in life was truly inspiring.

I sprinted off the two-lane road into the gravel parking area of the lodge. I checked the time on my watch as I struggled to catch my breath. I surveyed the spectacular beauty that surrounded me. Like a tidal wave of insight, it hit me. This was a picture of my life. Running. Running away. I fooled myself into thinking I was conquering life, winning at everything. I was not running to *anything.* I was running away . . . away from my kids, from my wife, my choices, my past . . . my pain . . . and I didn't even know it.

I started the short walk back to the cabin to get cleaned up. As I rounded the gear shed, Gabriel emerged from the woods. Just like I remembered him from the airport, he had on his knit cap, a worn-thin flannel shirt, and he was carrying a mug of coffee.

"Morning, Blake." He didn't stop walking and greeted me as he stroked his beard.

"Morning," I wheezed, still a little out of breath.

"I'd like to take you to a couple of places today. You in?"

"Oh yeah, what places?"

"You'll see." He smiled as he walked past me.

"We're not going over any waterfalls, are we?"

"Now that you mention it, that might be fun!" He kept walking.

"Seriously, what are you thinking?" I said louder as he got farther away.

He turned and started walking backward as he spoke with a devilish grin.

"Meet me at the Jeep in twenty minutes. Wear comfortable shoes, hiking boots if you have them." His deep, gravelly voice sounded like he'd smoked for years.

He faced back the other way and turned the corner at the gear shed.

What have I gotten myself into?

I had all kinds of questions running through my mind. Even though I didn't really know this guy, I trusted him. He had such a presence about him. Even when we talked in the airport that first time we met, I was hooked. He seemed like a man who was really alive. Not only was he alive, he was living for something and it was bigger than big.

We rambled along the winding road in his Jeep, my head bobbing with every grind of the gears. The roofless and rusted-out chassis made for a chilly ride.

"There's coffee in that thermos back there and plenty of snacks and such in the cooler."

"Coffee would be nice." I helped myself to the large army-green thermos. "So are you going to tell me where we are going?"

"Did you notice the canyon walls on these switchbacks? Amazing, aren't they?"

"Okay, okay. I'm just curious."

"You know sometimes we are so preoccupied with what's next that we miss spectacular moments on the journey. Look up that hill."

Gabriel pointed across me to the mountainside. A couple of hundred feet up the canyon wall was a majestic bighorn sheep perched on a giant boulder, keeping watch over the canyon.

"Wow. How in the world did that thing get up there? That is steep!"

"It's their hooves and sense of balance. They have these pads that grip the rock better than any climbing shoe. They can ascend to escape predators. Impressive animals."

I learned my lesson. I would just drink in the ride through the canyon and keep watch for more stunning discoveries. I gave myself over to the wonder of it all. We saw two bald eagles gliding overhead and a rattlesnake crossing the road. The road climbed and dipped through the canyon, The River nearly always in view, sometimes through the towering trees below, sometimes thundering a few feet away.

After about a forty-five minute drive, he pulled off the road and we bounced down a rugged path into the woods. The path ended into a densely treed ridge. We could hear the white noise of the white water nearby.

Gabriel jumped out of the Jeep and grabbed his backpack from behind his seat. He moved like a twenty-year-old.

"I'm going to take you to three places today, Blake. Three places that mean a great deal to me. Sometimes what we need in our lives is a little bit of perspective. Whenever I visit these places, I remember what's important."

Gabriel seemed to know that I needed more than just a little adventure; I needed a change.

I followed Gabriel into the woods. We walked along a narrow trail for about five minutes before we encountered the water.

"How's your balance?" Gabriel asked loudly over the white water's hushed growl.

"Pretty good, I think."

"Okay, stay close. It slopes down and it's a little wet from the spray." He grinned.

About ten feet over the white water, a fallen pine stretched out as a natural bridge to an island. When I got up close, it felt like a hundred feet up. The water cascading underneath gave the illusion that the ground was moving.

Gabriel took two steps out and bounced on it to make sure it was steady. He took one more step out over the water and then reached his arm back for me.

"I'm good," I said, waving him on. I prided myself on my athletic prowess. He inched out farther, holding his arms out like a high-wire circus performer, keeping his balance. He went all the way across without even a bobble.

It was my turn. I glanced at Gabriel as he was setting his backpack down on the other side of The River. He shot me a thumbs-up. He shouted something at me, but it was difficult to hear over the powerful river flow.

"What?" I yelled.

He cupped his hands and said it again, but I couldn't make it out.

I stepped out onto the log and pushed down to make sure of my footing. A few short steps and I was over the white water. I felt like I was flying as the water rushed underneath me. I looked up and smiled at Gabriel. He pointed to my feet. I took the next step and stumbled on a knot in the tree, and in the blink of an eye, I was dangling upside down like a sloth, hugging the tree for my life.

"Hold on, man!" I heard Gabriel yell. I could feel the mist of the water below on my neck as I struggled to get a grip. Before I knew it, he was out on the log just above me.

"Try to spin over on your belly!"

The moist algae made it very difficult to grip. I felt Gabriel grab the back of my jacket behind my shoulder. The power in his one arm was enough to pull me back up on the log and on my stomach. He started laughing.

"What are you laughing at!" I shouted with heightened urgency.

"The look on your face! Now, just crawl over on your belly."

He backed himself all the way across as I followed like a scared kitten, gripping the wet log with all my might.

"Maybe you should have taken my arm after all, huh?"

I glared at him as I wiped off the algae and soggy bark that covered my chest.

He took me down over the backside of the small island through a patch of trees and to an opening where a stack of large river rocks stood, like a monument in the middle of the wild.

"Is this what you told me about?" I asked.

"Welcome to The Stones of Remembrance."

I walked around to the front of the rocks and immediately looked to the bottom right corner. I knelt and scraped some of the dirt off the stone. I saw it with my own eyes. The symbol . . . the etching on the cornerstone he told me about. It was the symbol of The River. I ran my fingers over the grooves in the rock. A shiver went down my spine as I contemplated the history of this place.

"How long has this monument been here?"

"Jacob started the stacking at the time of my father's death which was 1956 . . . so fifty-six years or so."

I backed up and surveyed all the rocks that had been

stacked. It was well over my head now, eight or nine feet at least.

Gabriel walked up and pointed to a large one in the middle of the formation.

"This is my 'new beginnings' stone." He pointed to another. "This one I placed here when Rio went home. I've put more than thirty stones here over the years."

Gabriel placed his hand on the monument, his head bowed in reverence.

In that moment, I felt my own sense of loss, searching for something to anchor my existence. I was reeling inside at the thought of my wife of more than fifteen years, and the mother of my children, in pain at my choices. I thought of my kids and how I'd chased everything in life but my relationship with them. I was lost. As the weight of my situation became heavier, Gabriel opened a small leather-bound book. He sat down and began to read.

"From The Journal, book three:

It is important to remember. Remember those who have loved you well. Remember that even though you have made mistakes, you are not a mistake. Remember that forgiveness is waiting. Remember to forgive. Remember that it's never too late to love well. Remember that when you give yourself away, you never have need. Remember, The River is the center of all things, and as it flows, it carries with it new life."

He closed the book and looked back at the wall.

"Before I could really move forward in my life, I had to

remember to give thanks. I had to let go of some things. I needed to start the journey of forgiveness. I needed to ask for it, and I certainly needed to give it. I think of my father often and how he led a life of self-sacrifice to others, and ultimately exchanged his life for Jacob and the other kayaker. What could I hold on to? It's not easy, but I find freedom every time I let go."

My heart, my defenses were melting internally at Gabriel's words.

"Come here for a second." Gabriel gestured and walked to the tip of the island upstream covered with beautiful smooth stones. "Do you hear that?"

"It's the river stones . . . like marbles . . . They are getting worked over by The River, aren't they?" I said.

He held up a stunningly smooth stone the size of his palm. Its lavender, blue, and gray hues were laced in perfect circles. It looked like marble or granite.

"Every time I'm here, I stack a rough stone of remembrance, and I take a smooth stone from the water's edge. It reminds me of how being in The River has shaped me. It's making me a new man. My mistakes, my past are being tumbled into a new work of art."

He walked back over to the monument and reached into his backpack. He handed me an antiqued leather book. It had the symbol stamped on the front.

"What is this?"

"It's a river journal for you. You can start your own writings of what you hear The River say to you. It's blank, ready for you to fill the pages."

My heart lurched in my chest. "I don't know what to say."

I opened up the front cover and saw this inscription on the inside.

To my friend, Blake—When The River speaks, write it down. May these pages be filled with a life completely alive. For when you experience The River, you live!

Always in The River,

Gabriel Clarke

"Thank you so much, Gabriel."

"You're welcome. Before we go, I'd like you to do me a favor."

"Sure . . . anything."

"I want you to put a stone of remembrance on the monument. Before you do, I want you to write three things in that journal. First, I want you to write a message in the journal to your wife. Second, write one to your kids. Third, I want you to write a message to commemorate your stone of remembrance."

Gabriel smiled like a gentle father, handed me a pen, and walked away.

I felt as though my soul was laid bare in this moment, and I hadn't really told him the full story.

I sat down and opened the blank journal. I'll never forget the feeling of the tears tumbling down my cheek and staining the page as I wrote.

Dear Sarah,

I'm not worthy of your love. I'm so sorry. I'm so sorry I hurt you. I was wrong. You don't deserve this. My heart aches for you. I'm sorry for letting you down. I'm sorry for neglecting you and going my own way. I don't even know why I did it, why I let my heart wander. I miss your smile. I miss laughing with you at the funny things the kids say. Nothing is right without you. Nothing. Please give me another chance. I'll do whatever it takes. Whatever you want, to be with you again.

—Blake

Dear Jake, Lily, and Dylan,

I want you to know that I love you very much. I miss you. There's a better way to live than what I've shown you. It's not about what you have, but who you are. I haven't said it very much, but I'm so proud of all of you. I want to spend more time with you in the coming days. Being your dad is the best thing in the world.

I love you all.

—Dad

I hereby lay this stone to remember this day, October 4, 2012, as a day of turning. Today I turn away from my empty, selfish ways, and I turn toward my family and those I've been given to love. I have been blessed beyond measure, and I vow to never take them for granted again. May this stone be a memorial to everything The River is showing me.

—Blake Caruthers

The rock I placed on the monument that day was heavy . . . a feather compared to my sorrow. Gabriel and I left The Stones of Remembrance, and I felt a glimmer of hope. Today I had exchanged a piece of the old me for the hope of what could be. She might not take me back . . . I knew that. I held on to hope.

Gabriel and I made our way across the tree bridge and back to the Jeep. We went back to the lodge for the evening, and he continued to share his journey with me before he took me to the second unforgettable place.

15

A Surprising Encounter

September 28, 1973—4:00 p.m. at the Lodge

Gabriel's first season as a rafting guide came to a close in early September of '73. The season proved to be rich with unforgettable times on the water, life-changing conversations with Ezra, and the love he and Tabitha shared running more deeply than ever.

The fall mountain air felt fresh and cold as Gabriel finished the last corner of the gear shed with wood stain. The camp had been closed for weeks now, and most of the seasonal team had gone back to their hometowns. Gabriel, Tabitha, Jacob, Sadie, and Ezra all lived at The River year-round.

"Dad's up in the office. I'm going to go take a nap. There're some leftovers in the kitchen from lunch." Tabitha pressed a quick kiss on Gabriel's scruffy cheek.

"Thanks. I think I'm going to go for a hike . . . maybe up to the Cathedral."

"It's going to be dark soon so be careful," Tabitha said as she walked away.

Gabriel put away his paintbrush and stain can and went back to his cabin to get his backpack and supplies. He donned his army-green knit cap and gray wool turtleneck.

The crunching of his boots on the earth and the pulse of his exhale was all he could hear on the quiet canyon trail. The late-afternoon twilight made the canyon look a blue-gray tint. On his final few steps into the clearing, two little creatures scampered through his peripheral vision. He glanced over to see the little chipmunks scouring the forest floor for a few more nuts before winter. His mind raced back to his first big hike with his father. He smiled to himself as he reminisced softly.

"Nuts and Pea. I guess you guys never left, huh?"

They scurried back into the woods and peeked out from behind the giant firs.

He thought about riding his dad's shoulders up into the woods that day. He remembered naming the scurrying chipmunks and the feel of his dad's hair in his hands as he held on. He pictured the game of marbles overlooking The River and the last image of his father's face glancing up at him before he went in after the kayaker . . . after Jacob.

Gabriel arrived at the first of two stops on his hike, the area of Splashfire, where his life changed forever. He slowly made his way to the ridge and placed his hand on the tree with The River symbol of Ama-Woya. He looked to the bottom of the thunderous falls where his father went into The

River forever. In his heart, he knew he had begun to embrace the power of his father's sacrifice saving Jacob. He watched the white-water mist rising from the great waterfall. A small break in the gray twilight let the last bit of the sun's rays through, and a prism of light, a rainbow, shown beautifully against the backdrop of the canyon wall. As the thick mist melted into the air, he imagined the mist as the spirit of his father, John Clarke, rising up from the waters into the sky. Gabriel placed his hand on his heart, then on the symbol. Each time he visited the site, little by little, he felt the crushing weight of his grief and anger giving way to gratitude and peace. He picked up his backpack and headed back down the path. At the fork, he made the turn and ascended to the Cathedral of the Sun to visit his father . . . and Rio.

As Gabriel rounded the last bend in the path, he was startled to see a man sitting on the ground with his back to him, facing his dad's gravesite. He wore a black knit cap on his head and a red jacket. The man startled and spun his head around as he heard Gabriel's footsteps approach. Gabriel's heart skipped a beat. It was Billy Fielding. His dark brow was furrowed and his eyes were tired and puffy. His dark beard was long.

Gabriel stopped in his tracks.

"How's it going?" Gabriel said cautiously.

"I've been better," Billy said calmly.

"It's a cold one today," Gabriel replied.

It occurred to Gabriel, due to Billy's drunken state that day, he might not even remember him from that volatile encounter a few months ago.

"What brings you up here?" Gabriel asked.

"Paying my respects." Billy stood up and dusted off his jeans.

Gabriel approached him slowly. They both stared down at Gabriel's father's grave.

"So did you know John Clarke?" Gabriel asked.

"Not really. I know he was a hero . . . a legend."

"Do you come here often?"

"When I can. Did you know him?"

"Yes, but not for long. So you live close by?"

"Yeah. I have a place not too far from here back in the woods. It's pretty much just me and The River," Billy said as he perused the view over the water.

"What kind of work do you do?"

"I'm a handyman, I guess. I like to work with wood too. Used to be a white-water guide."

"That's what I do," Gabriel said confidently.

"So you said you knew him, but not for long?"

"John Clarke is my father . . . was my father. I'm Gabriel Clarke."

Billy looked at Gabriel as if he'd seen a ghost.

"I better be getting back," Billy said nervously.

He slung his backpack on his shoulders and started to walk away.

"Hey, wait," Gabriel said quickly.

"Yeah?" Billy looked back over his shoulder.

"I've got some jerky in my pack. You want some?"

"I'm good, thanks anyway." He turned and kept walking.

"Jacob said you were amazing on The River."

Billy stopped. He turned around.

"Jacob who?"

"Jacob Fielding . . . your brother."

"What makes you think I have a brother?"

"Jacob would really like to see you again. He told me you guys ran The River together for years."

"He said that?"

"Yeah. Many times. He's taught me a lot about The River."

"I'm surprised you'll have anything to do with him." Billy walked back toward Gabriel with a questioning look.

"Why is that?"

Billy swallowed hard as he continued. "After what we did? We shouldn't have been out there that day."

Gabriel started to put it together. His mind's eye flashed back. There were two kayakers that day. His focus had been solely on his relationship with Jacob.

"You were the other kayaker?"

Billy nodded.

"You were the one Dad was able to warn in time." He recalled more. "You didn't go over the falls. I remember. You gave Jacob CPR."

"I gotta go." Billy turned quickly.

"Hey, can we talk some more?"

"About what?"

"I would really like to remember more about that day. You're the only other one who was there."

Billy reluctantly came back, and the two men sat down on a fallen tree facing The River.

Gabriel spoke first.

"My last memory is Dad's hand reaching out of the water, and then I saw you scrambling to get to Jacob, pulling him up on that rock and giving him CPR. What happened after that? I don't remember much of anything until Kansas."

Gabriel passed Billy a piece of jerky from his backpack.

The forty-something man sat with his elbows on his knees as he took a bite and reminisced.

"I thought I'd lost Jacob. We were so careless. God, he was so blue. It was a miracle that he survived. I had to tie up his shoulder. The blood was just pouring out. Once I got a pulse on him, I heard this kid—you—screaming up on the ridge, alone." He took off his knit cap and ran his fingers through his jet-black oily hair. "You were terrified and confused. What little kid wouldn't be? I left Jacob there and crossed downstream. I asked you what your name was, and you just stared at me. I tried to get you to come with me to the other side so I could watch out for you. You wouldn't let go of the tree." Billy's lip quivered and his voice cracked. He stared at the dirt.

"'Where is my dad? Where is my dad?' you kept asking me. It was like a dagger through my heart." He wiped his nose with his hand. The power of the memory overtook him. His face turned red, veins popping as he tried to keep from sobbing. "Man, I'm sorry."

Gabriel sat calmly for a moment as he processed Billy's emotion. He felt sorry for him. He didn't know what to say. He knew he had every right to be angry at the man, but he wasn't. His compassion for this broken man outweighed the memory of what he did.

"So it's pretty cool that my dad caught your attention before you went over the falls, huh?"

Billy nodded.

"I'm coming to terms with everything, Billy. I still get angry from time to time . . . sad too. But I'm moving further away from it. New memories are pushing out the old. My dad was a great man. He's not here. Now it's time for us to get on with being great men."

Billy composed himself. The grace Gabriel extended him in that moment brought visible relief.

"There was a hiker nearby who really saved the day for us. He stayed with Jacob while I carried you out of the gorge and went for help. I delivered you to your mother back at the lodge. I went back with the paramedics and officers to get Jacob out."

"When did they get my father's body out?"

"We found the body that afternoon downstream."

Gabriel had memory flashes . . . scenes he hadn't remembered that ran through his mind . . . his mother taking him from Billy . . . Billy carrying him out of the canyon . . . then . . . his view at the funeral.

"Were you at the funeral?"

"No . . . I was too ashamed. I heard the whole town showed up. I wish now that I would have gone."

Gabriel's newly recalled memories became more vivid. He saw the casket with the white-water helmet and paddle resting on top. He remembered sitting on his mother's lap and her whispering in his ear, "I love you, baby." He saw Ezra reading from a book next to his father's body.

"It helps to hear some of this. It feels like a few more pieces to the puzzle of my life are getting filled in." Gabriel changed the subject. "Why aren't you and Jacob on good terms?"

"Just too much has happened. You don't know me. You don't know my past."

Gabriel felt himself stepping out of his introversion to reach into Billy's world.

"Everyone has a past."

"Not everyone has a past like mine."

"Can you tell me about it?"

He shook his head.

"I'm sure Jacob will tell you. I better be getting back." Billy stood up.

"Hey . . . for what it's worth, he wants you to come home again. I think he really misses you."

"That's funny. Never heard him say that. Glad you're doing well, Gabriel Clarke."

"Billy."

"Yeah." The mountain man squinted as he looked at Gabriel.

"Thanks for taking me off the mountain that day."

Billy nodded, took one more look at John Clarke's gravestone, and then reached into his backpack and rifled through it until he pulled out an envelope.

"Here. You should have this," Billy said and then disappeared into the woods.

Gabriel opened the dirty envelope and pulled out the tattered, folded newspaper clipping inside. He unfolded it gently. He read the headline.

"Local hero dies saving two brothers."

Below the headline . . . a picture of his father . . . smiling . . . holding young Gabriel.

Gabriel looked up to see if he could catch Billy, but he

was gone. Gabriel sat back down and read every word of the article, chronicling the heroic efforts of his father. As hard as it was to see and read the account again, he knew he held a treasure in his hand.

Gabriel got up and went over to a large pile of river stones that lay next to the Cathedral rock. He knelt down and placed his hand on them.

"My Rio. Hey, buddy. I've missed you. It's not the same around the camp without you. Would you see if there're any others like you up there and send me another friend?" He laid a piece of jerky on the stones. "It's teriyaki. Your favorite." He smiled.

As Gabriel left the Cathedral of the Sun, his heart was heavy for Billy. These two brothers were in his life—each of them seemed to live with their pain differently. One appeared free. One seemed shackled.

He was grateful that instead of memories feeling like a crushing weight, they were beginning to lift him, like stepping-stones to a free and whole-hearted existence. He was learning each day that a greater story was unfolding and The River was at the center . . . not him.

16

Millie

November 1973

"Thanks for coming, Ezra." Jacob turned to his mentor in the passenger seat.

"Of course," Ezra replied as the Jeep chugged up the winding roads.

The light snowfall coated the road in a soft, white blanket. The pines and firs dusted with the powder turned the canyon into a winter wonderland under the gray sky canopy.

Gabriel piped up from the backseat as he wiped the fog from the clear plastic window of the soft top. "The snow seems to quiet everything down. It's really beautiful."

They crested a hill and started to descend on a tight switchback. Jacob downshifted and the back of the Jeep slid a little.

"Whoa." Gabriel gripped the roll bar. Ezra didn't flinch.

"Yeah, we don't want to end up down there." Jacob chuckled as he looked out his window at the steep drop-off just a few feet away. He pulled off the road onto an unmarked, snow-covered path.

"I don't know how you do it," Gabriel said to Jacob.

"Do what?"

"Know where you're going out here, especially in the snow. Everything seems to change in the snow. I don't have a clue where we are."

"I've just been here so many years, I guess I have a feel for it," Jacob replied with confidence.

Ezra started a slow, rumbling laugh.

"What's so funny?" Jacob sounded defensive.

"Oh nothin'." Ezra tried to gain his composure.

"Come on, Ezra. You can tell me," Gabriel said, smiling.

"Well, I guess it's just years of Jacob's experience that helped him know the path. Here I thought it was just that red rag tied up in that pine."

"I didn't see that . . . I just knew." Jacob was smiling now. "Why do you have to give away all my secrets, Ezra?"

"Oh, I see!" Gabriel flicked Jacob in the shoulder and laughed.

Jacob set the parking break on the Jeep and jumped out to turn the hubs for four-wheel drive. He got back in, rubbing his hands together vigorously. "I guess it's officially winter."

Before he began the rocky descent to Billy's cabin, he paused.

"I hope we find him here. It's been too long."

The Jeep descended the hill slowly. They parked among the trees where the ground leveled. Snow covered the tin roof of the small wood cabin, and smoke billowed from the chimney. Billy's truck sat parked a few feet away. Jacob led the way with Gabriel and Ezra a few steps behind. He walked up on the porch and knocked on the wood plank door.

"Billy. It's Jacob."

He knocked again.

No answer.

He formed a visor with his hands and peered in the window. The fire was going in the potbelly stove, and a couple of lamps were on.

"I'll go check around back." Gabriel zipped up his coat and flipped his collar up to keep warm. His boots squeaked against the snow as it melted under each step. He walked around the back of the cabin and made his way toward a large wooden shed where a door was cracked open.

"Billy?" Gabriel approached the shed and pulled the door open gently. He heard a scraping sound. He poked his head in. He noticed a large table saw with lots of woodworking tools lying around. Some of them looked familiar . . . maybe from Jacob's collection. A solitary work light dangled from the ceiling. The sawdust smelled fresh. Gabriel opened the door farther and walked in.

His pulse quickened at the eerie silence. After a few seconds, he walked back outside. He'd taken a couple of steps when he noticed boot impressions in the snow that led into the woods. They were fresh but fading fast. Without thinking, Gabriel followed the footprints. The forest grew more dense with each tromp of his boot. He glanced back toward the cabin before the prints took a turn toward The River. *Is this a good idea?* His exhales steamed in the sub-freezing temperature. If he went back to get Jacob, he might lose the prints. With his eyes glued to the footprints as they grew more and more faint, he lifted his head and saw what appeared to be Billy about twenty yards away. He was on his knees in the snow. His knit cap was almost entirely covered with snow. He sat staring at something on the ground. As Gabriel got closer, he broke the silence.

"Billy?"

The bearded man didn't respond.

Gabriel saw what he was staring at . . . a small wooden box resting at the foot of a large spruce tree.

"Hey, Billy. Me and Jacob and Ezra came to see you. They're back at your cabin."

Billy turned to look at Gabriel slowly. His cheeks were wet with tears.

"She would have been fourteen today. I made this box for a couple of things I found of hers."

Gabriel didn't know what to say. He looked over his shoulder and saw Jacob and Ezra approaching. They joined at his side.

"I only turned around for a few moments, Jacob . . . it was only a few moments," Billy said as he put his head in his hands and sobbed. "It's my fault! It's my fault!" he kept saying through his cries.

Ezra walked over, stood next to Billy, and put one hand on his shoulder.

Jacob tried to comfort his brother. "Billy, don't say that. Don't say that. It could have happened to anyone."

The grief-stricken man tried to compose himself as he continued telling the story. "The water was so high that day . . . We didn't know it was going to flood the canyon like it did. We were watching The River from the porch. The rain was pouring down like I'd never seen it." He laughed through his tears as he remembered. "That little girl had no fear. We were all just praying for it to stop, and she kept asking to go out to play in it. She'd never really wandered off the porch before. I went in to taste that pot roast Janie was cooking. I didn't think I was gone long enough for her to make it to the water's edge."

His eyes opened wide and he looked at Jacob as if something new came to his memory.

"I was drinking, Jacob. I was drinking!" he shouted. "What kind of man leaves his daughter alone?"

He started to break again. "All these years, wondering when I would find her. I saw you fishing that day. I saw that you found her. I wanted to bring her back here, back home." He looked back down at the ground. "I'm sorry, Millie. I'm so sorry."

Dusk was settling on the canyon. The snowflakes got larger and more numerous. Gabriel felt Billy's pain deeply. If there's one thing he knew, it was debilitating grief. A sadness that is so crushingly heavy you can barely breathe. He felt for many years that he should have been able to save his dad that fateful day. He carried guilt for years for staying glued to the tree. He was only five, but that didn't matter. He felt he should've tried to save him. He watched Billy writhe in agony at losing his little girl, and he longed to offer some help. All he knew to do was just be there.

The men waited in silence, standing guard as Billy grieved. Gabriel joined in his tears. After several minutes passed and night grew closer, Ezra sensed the rest in Billy and jumped into bring a little levity to a dark situation.

"Boys, I'm not sure if I have any toes. If I do . . . and I pray that I do . . . I sure can't feel 'em. How about I make everyone some hot chocolate?"

Gabriel and Jacob smiled. Billy wiped his nose and stood to his feet. Jacob pulled him into a bear hug. "You can get through this. We'll get through this," Jacob said quietly.

The four men lumbered together through the snow back to the rustic cabin. Jacob put his arm around Billy's shoulder as they walked. "The three of us ought to go out on the water come spring," Jacob said as he looked at Gabriel and Billy.

"Sounds great to me," Gabriel replied as he headed to grab some logs from a cord of wood that was stacked against the back of the house to stoke the fire in the claw foot potbelly stove. They took off their gloves and laid them on the ground next to the stove to warm them. They all sat around the rough-hewn, round farm table in the kitchen as Ezra worked his magic with the supplies he had brought.

"Gentlemen, is anyone in the mood to lose some money?" Jacob took a deck of cards out of his coat pocket and slapped them on the table.

Gabriel tapped his finger to his chin and assumed a puzzled expression. "Do you guys hear that?" Gabriel cupped his hand to his ear.

"What?" Jacob responded.

Billy glanced up.

Gabriel answered his own question. "Yep. I hear it. It's the sound of Jacob putting cash into my hand. Jacob, save yourself the trouble, and go ahead and give me all your money."

Jacob snickered. "Oh, I see. I see. Billy, you in?"

"Why not?"

"Ezra, how 'bout you?" Jacob looked back at the old man at the stove who was stirring his chocolaty brew in a large saucepan.

"Do you promise to take it easy on the old man? I'm not as sharp as I used to be." Ezra pulled the spoon up to his mouth for a taste. His hand shook a bit.

Gabriel commented to Billy under his breath, "Don't believe that slow Southern drawl for a second. He's a sand-bagger . . . wins at everything. Show no mercy. He'll start moving slower . . . talking slower. You watch. It's quite impressive, actually."

They settled in around the table with their mugs of rich hot chocolate, and Jacob dealt the cards.

"What are we betting?" Billy asked.

Jacob reached in his other pocket and pulled out a huge roll of one-dollar bills held together with a rubber band.

"What do you think? There's four hundred here. I was going to use this for some bills, but I think this is a better idea. Gabriel, I owe you some money for those extra hours. Ezra, I'm sure I owe you from previous games, and, Billy . . . you're my brother, so why not? Each of us gets a hundred." He snapped the rubber band off and divvied up the loot.

Ezra took a pipe out of his jacket pocket and showed it to Billy.

"Do you mind?"

"Not at all, Ezra."

He pulled out a tin of tobacco and began to stuff the pipe slowly.

"Texas hold 'em, boys." Jacob slid the cards to each man.

Billy seemed to be loosening up. "Jacob, do you remember when we were kids and we decided to hang that rope swing over Jamison Creek?"

"I don't know what you're talking about." Jacob dismissed it as he looked at his cards.

Billy turned to Gabriel and Ezra.

"I think Jacob was about thirteen, and I was ten. He was always trying to impress the girls. So Sally Culverson came with us to the creek, and Jacob wanted to try a fancy swing into the water. So he climbs way up the tree to launch himself out, but it was never good enough for Jacob to just swing normally; he had to turn it into a trick." Billy stood up, acting out the moves. "He twists his foot around the rope and starts to swing upside down, only his foot slipped, and somehow his pants got caught on the rope, and as he slid down, his pants didn't! There he was, hanging bare-butt from a rope swinging across the creek. Full moon! Sally Culverson got more than she bargained for that day!"

Jacob sat there shaking his head and looking at his cards. He couldn't help but join the laughter.

"I don't remember seeing Sally after that." Jacob shrugged his shoulders.

"I'm out." Gabriel laid his cards down.

"Why don't you come work with us again?" Jacob asked his younger brother.

Billy seemed hesitant. "I've got some other jobs to do. I don't know. Ezra?"

"Call," the old man said as he blew smoke from the corner of his mouth and kept the game going. They laid their cards down. Ezra waited a moment, then laid down his. "Are these any good?" he asked, sounding naive.

"Aw, man! Are you kidding me? A royal flush?" Jacob yelled in frustration.

Ezra smiled as he scooped the pile of one-dollar bills over to himself.

"I was running a little low on tobacco, so this will come in handy. Thank you, boys."

"I told you . . . the luckiest man alive!" Gabriel pointed at Ezra.

Ezra spoke up again. "You know, our evening together made me think of something." Ezra took out a small leather-bound book from his jacket pocket. He sorted through the pages and stopped. "Ah-ha. Here it is. I wrote this down many years ago in my journal." He read aloud.

Sometimes life takes us to our purpose and destiny the long way 'round. The Maker sees the end from the beginning all at once. The timing doesn't make sense to us, but from a higher view, it is right. It will be right. In the season of the long and dark valley, the soil of our lives becomes rich and fertile with the nutrients of our suffering. That soil, the soil of suffering, grows trees that bear the most luscious fruit . . . flowers that bloom in colors so vivid we can't even describe it . . . and joy that can never be taken away . . . if we will allow it. So take heart and know that your tears are shared, and one day, you will laugh again.

Ezra closed his book and slid it back down into his jacket pocket as he continued.

"I never had any children. But you boys are like my sons. I want you to listen to me." The three men didn't say a word as Ezra made eye contact with each one of them. "Don't let what happened tonight disappear. Friendship. Respect. Honor. Joy. Forgiveness . . . and above all, love. Take it from an old man. Life is very short. Don't waste another moment without each other."

A banging on the door crashed in on the moment. Billy slid his chair out quickly and walked over to open it. Gabriel was shocked to see Freddie standing there.

"Freddie, what's wrong?" Gabriel saw the panic on his face.

"You guys gotta come quick. It's Tabitha . . . she . . . she fell . . . Hurt herself pretty bad, I think."

Gabriel's brain saw stars, but his body leaped into action. The men grabbed their coats and rushed to the Jeep.

17

The Scare

Due to snow accumulation, the trip back to the lodge took them twice as long as before. Gabriel's heart convulsed in his chest as the unthinkable what-ifs raced through his mind.

What if I lose her? Will she be okay?

Both Jeeps slid into the lodge parking area after an hour of dicey maneuvering through the canyon. Gabriel and Jacob jumped out and rushed up the lodge steps and through the door. They ran into the back living area next to the dining room. Tabitha was stretched out on her back on the avocado-green tweed sofa with an ice pack resting on her head and a large bandage on her left thigh. Sadie greeted them.

"She was heading over to your cabin, Gabriel. She wanted to leave some treats she baked for you. I knew it had taken her too long, so I went out to check on her, and she was on the ground. She doesn't remember what happened, but by the looks of it, she slipped on a patch of ice. She said her head was hurting pretty bad. She's got a nasty gash on her leg from a rock as well."

Gabriel shook his head in disbelief. He sat down next to her and picked up her hand. She opened her eyes just enough to see and smiled.

"Hey, you," she said in a tired slur.

"Hey. How are you feeling?"

"I'm okay, just a little foggy. I'm such a klutz."

Gabriel looked at Sadie. "Did she lose consciousness?"

"I'm not sure. When I found her, she was sitting up, just a little dazed."

Ezra finally made it to the room and saw that Tabitha was okay. He breathed a huge sigh of relief.

"Thanks for coming to get us, Freddie," Jacob said as he rubbed his hands over his tired eyes. "I'm really glad it's not as bad as your face made it seem." Jacob looked at Freddie with a bit of exasperation.

"I was worried!" Freddie defended.

Jacob nodded. "I know. I know. You did the right thing."

"That girl has been giving me heart attacks since she was a little one." Ezra threw up his hands and walked into the kitchen. "I'll make us some tea."

"Let me check that leg." Gabriel lifted the bandage up gently on her lower left thigh. "Did you guys clean this out? It's pretty deep and jagged."

"Not yet. We just wanted to stop the bleeding and get her comfortable," Sadie responded.

"You're definitely going to need some stitches." Gabriel got up to get some peroxide and first-aid supplies.

"I'll be fine. I just want to go to bed." Tabitha started to sit up.

Gabriel took her gently by the shoulders.

"It won't take but a minute. I'll clean it up and then you can get some sleep. I'll take you into town in the morning to get you stitched up. Hopefully the snow will have stopped and the roads will be better then."

She let him lay her back down and adjust the ice pack under her head.

Gabriel joined Jacob in the back office to fetch the peroxide and bandages.

"That first-aid training is coming in handy, huh?" Jacob noticed Gabriel's initiative. "Don't let her talk you out of help. She always thinks she can handle it."

"I won't. She's feisty, alright."

After having her wound cleaned, Tabitha seemed even more exhausted. "I'm going to bed," she declared as she stood up on her right leg. She immediately lost her balance and grabbed Gabriel's arm. "Just a little dizzy."

"Okay, that's enough." Gabriel lifted her up with ease, cradling her in his arms, gently avoiding the cut on her leg. "I've got you." She wrapped her arms around his neck and rested her head on his shoulder.

"I'll get her bed ready." Sadie led the way down the hall and up the stairs to Tabitha's bedroom.

Gabriel navigated the narrow wooden stairs gingerly, not wanting to bang her head or leg on anything.

Sadie propped the pillows up and pulled the handmade

quilts back on the bed. Gabriel laid her down softly onto her bed, and Sadie untied Tabitha's boots, removed them, and peeled off her socks.

Gabriel took a few steps back and looked around the room. He'd never been in there. He'd never even been in a girl's room before. It smelled like her. He noticed one of his favorite sweaters that she wore draped over her wrought-iron footboard. The lava lamp on her nightstand bubbled next to a picture of her and Gabriel by The River. He recognized a stack of notes that he had written her lying on her dresser next to her hairbrush. Several pictures of fun days on the water with river runners were tucked in the bottom of her dresser mirror. Another picture wedged in the top right corner took him by surprise. It was a small sepia-tone wallet-size picture of his dad holding him when he was just a boy.

He turned his attention back to Tabitha as Sadie kept getting her settled in.

"Gabriel, could you hand me that . . . hanging on the closet door?" Tabitha pointed from her bed.

Gabriel grabbed the thin flannel nightshirt and handed it to Sadie.

"I think this is where you leave," Sadie said protectively.

"Are you sure? You might need help. I can close my eyes." He flashed a devilish grin.

"Good night," the little blonde said as she raised her eyebrows and showed him out the door.

"Thank you, Gabriel." Tabitha waved from her bed.

"Sleep well. I'll see you in the morning."

He backed out the door, keeping his eyes glued to her all

the way. He closed it gently and went back down the steps to the living area. The others must have all headed to bed as well. He arranged the pillows on the couch, then plopped down in the large brown leather poet's chair in the corner. As the snow floated silently outside, he thought about how relieved he was that she was okay. In those long moments when he didn't know how hurt she was, he realized he couldn't bear to be without her. He reached behind and grabbed the large afghan draped over the back of the chair and covered his legs. He leaned back and rehearsed in his mind every memory of them together he could recall.

The time he saw her climb out of that van on his first trip to The River . . . Their conversations under the stars on The Beach or the red-tailed hawk . . . His first time on the big water or her tricking him to jump off The Cliffs . . . Even the times of great difficulty, she was there.

She helped him come alive. Her love reached deep into the quicksand of his inward-bent, fearful, and grieving heart. Her tenacity, her unselfish and generous spirit, got him to experience the one thing that would give him life, The River. This girl changed everything for Gabriel. He never knew he could love and be loved like this. He prayed it would never end.

Gabriel awoke with squinted eyes to the sound of pots clanging in the kitchen and a blinding reflection of the sun coming through the window.

"Did you stay there all night?" Sadie questioned as she

tied her flannel robe while shuffling down the hall in her fur slippers.

"I just wanted to be close in case she needed anything," Gabriel said as he rubbed his eyes with his knuckles.

"Well, that's sweet," Sadie replied.

Gabriel got up and laid the afghan back across the chair.

"You just never know what's going to happen out here. You think things are coasting along just fine and then . . . it never fails . . . the other shoe drops," Gabriel said.

Sadie looked at him.

"Yeah, I'm over it. I'm just over it. There's just too much that can happen, you know? Sometimes I just want something else . . . something more predictable . . . more safe," Sadie replied.

"Does that exist?" Gabriel asked.

"It has to," she answered.

"Is that the momma grizzly bear incident talking?" he asked her.

"I'd give anything to get rid of the awful dreams," she said, sounding frustrated.

The back door slammed.

"Good morning, Ezra," Gabriel said.

"Good morning. Pancakes and bacon sound good?" the old man asked as he made his way to the pantry.

"Absolutely, let me help you. I'll make Tabitha those cinnamon apple ones she likes," Gabriel said as he went into the kitchen.

"Oh yes. The apple butter is right in here and the cinnamon is in the spice rack over there," Ezra said as he pointed.

The smell of percolating coffee and sizzling smoked

bacon filled the lodge. Gabriel grabbed a tray and put two pancakes and bacon on her favorite plate and added some orange juice and coffee.

"Sadie, I'd like to take this up to her. Can you make sure the coast is clear?"

Sadie finished chewing her bite and wiped her mouth. "Yeah, sure."

She walked up the stairs and Gabriel followed. She went in and pushed the door closed behind her. Gabriel heard them talking for a few seconds, then Sadie came out.

"You're clear."

Gabriel walked in with the tray to see Tabitha sitting up in her bed, running her fingers through her hair in what was probably a last-ditch effort to look fresh.

"How are you feeling?"

"I'm okay. What are you doing? You are spoiling me."

"I made the apple cinnamon ones you like."

He set the tray down on her nightstand.

"Oh my gosh, that smells so good."

"Please don't do that again."

"Do what?"

"Practice your ballet on the ice."

"Ha-ha," she said sarcastically.

"I was really worried about you." His eyes met hers. "When you're done eating, I'm going to take you into town to get that cut taken care of."

"So, you slept in the chair downstairs last night?" she asked with affection.

"Yeah, just in case you needed anything. Let me know when you're done and I'll come get you." Gabriel leaned down and kissed her on the forehead. She took his hand in hers.

"Thank you."

"Enjoy your breakfast." He smiled and left the room.

———⊙———

Gabriel and Tabitha returned from town later that afternoon. She was able to walk with a slight limp but had to be careful on the snow and ice. Gabriel helped her into the lodge.

"Well, what did they say?" Jacob asked as he came in from the back office.

"A pretty good concussion and a couple dozen stitches. She just needs to rest for a while. I told her to practice her dance moves inside next time."

Tabitha rolled her eyes.

"Do you need anything?" Gabriel turned his attention to her again.

"No, just a nap."

"Okay, I'm going to go back to my room for a bit. I'll come check on you at dinner."

Gabriel climbed the steps to the porch of their cabin to hear Ezra coughing loudly through his closed door. He leaned his ear closer. The coughing got louder and more violent. He knocked.

"Ezra? Ezra, you okay in there?"

The coughing continued.

Concerned, Gabriel cracked Ezra's door open.

"Hey, are you okay?"

Ezra looked at Gabriel as he coughed again. He put his hand on his chest.

"I'll be fine," he said as he took a handkerchief out of his pocket and wiped his mouth.

"That didn't sound too good."

"That's the sound of being on the planet a long time." Ezra smiled warmly. "Come in here and sit down. I want to show you something."

Gabriel sat down on the edge of the perfectly made twin bed. Ezra walked over to his solitary chest of drawers and pulled the top one out.

"I hope we are done with all the excitement for a little while," Ezra commented.

"Yeah, that's not the kind of excitement I care to experience."

Ezra sat down beside Gabriel holding a faded picture. "I came across this the other day and thought you should have it."

Gabriel took it into his hands, speechless.

Ezra leaned in and pointed. "There's your dad and mom. You were only a few months old. Look at that face of yours."

"Mom looks absolutely beautiful. I've never seen them in a picture together."

In an instant, Gabriel thought about what it would have been like to grow up at The River, with both of them.

"Where was this taken?"

"I think it was right down by The Reflection Pool."

"So I can keep this?"

"Absolutely."

Gabriel stared at the sepia-toned image.

"I'm not sure how or why Mom went back to Kansas when I was little. All I know is, what I see in this picture right here . . . that's what I want. They are together here. That's how it should be. I don't want to do life alone, ya know? I'm going to build something for the future, Ezra."

"Are you saying what I think you're saying, son?" Ezra grinned.

"I usually don't have to tell you what I'm thinking. Guess you'll have to wait and see." Gabriel grinned as he winked.

18

A Road Trip

Early Spring, 1974

"Hello?" The female voice sounded tired.

"Mom?"

"Gabriel, is that you? I can't believe it's you! How are you?"

"I'm doing really well, Mom . . . really well."

"I was wondering if you were ever going to call. I've been worried about you."

"I know. I know. Life at The River has been amazing. I have so much to tell you. You know I'm not great at talking on the phone."

"I don't care if you're good at it. I just want to hear your voice," his mom, Maggie, said.

"Okay, okay, Mom."

"What about that girl you mentioned to me before? You spending any time with her these days?"

"Yeah, Mom. Her name is Tabitha and she's amazing." Gabriel shot a grin to Tabitha who was sitting next to him in the office. "I want you to meet her sometime. So you have a big day next week, huh?"

"What are you talking about?" She sounded confused.

"Mom. Your birthday?"

"Oh yeah, that. I'm getting less and less excited about those."

"You going to do anything fun?"

"I'll probably work, bake a pie, eat it, and that'll be the end of it." Maggie chuckled.

"Well, I hope it's a great day for you. You deserve it." He paused. "Well, I've got to get back to work on some things here."

"Okay, honey. Thanks for calling. I always love hearing from you. Please be careful . . . Oh, and come visit me sometime. I want to see your face."

"I will, Mom . . . maybe in a few months."

"I love you, sweetheart."

"Love you too, Mom."

Gabriel hung up the phone and looked at Tabitha.

"That wasn't too painful. She really lets me have it sometimes." Gabriel rolled his eyes and smiled. "I have an idea," he continued.

"Me too," she said as she snuggled in close and kissed his neck.

He squirmed at the thought of Jacob walking in on them in the office. "I do like your idea, but I have another."

"What's that?" she asked as she kissed him again.

"Let's surprise my mom for her birthday. I want you to go to Kansas with me for a few days. I want you to meet her."

Tabitha sat up. "Really?"

"Yeah, let's take a road trip, just you and me. Camp doesn't open for a few more weeks. Things are quiet around here. Will you come with me?" he asked as he held her shoulders in his hands. "Ms. Vonda, Mister Earl's wife, you know the family whose farm we lived on, she makes some amazing fried chicken."

"Uh, okay. Yeah, let's do it. I want to see where you grew up," she said as she smiled.

"Go where?" Jacob's strong voice burst into their moment as he entered the back of the office.

Tabitha jerked back from Gabriel's embrace.

"You scared me, Dad!"

"Good!" Jacob smiled.

Gabriel fidgeted to cover his embarrassment. "Jacob, I was going to ask you about going to surprise my mom for her birthday next week. I haven't seen her for a long time. I'd love it if Tabitha could go with me to meet her."

Jacob raised his eyebrows but nodded. "I see. I suppose we can manage around here for a few days."

The winters could be quite long in Colorado, which made the awakening of spring that much more enrapturing. The sleeping flowers and trees burst forth, painting the landscape with vivid washes of every color. The wildlife was more boisterous and active again, and the spring sun warmed the mornings earlier and earlier. The signs of life called everyone and everything out of its wintery rest to create, experience, and explore. Gabriel noticed this awakening in nature and felt his own sense of adventure as he and Tabitha were taking big steps in their relationship together.

Gabriel and Tabitha loaded up his old two-tone stepside pickup and started the day-and-a-half trek just after lunch on a warm and sunny Tuesday. They had a cooler full of sodas, sandwiches, and a small basket full of Ezra's cinnamon rolls, prepared fresh for them that morning. Sadie, Jacob, and Ezra all waved good-bye from the lodge deck as they rumbled out of the gravel drive.

Tabitha and Gabriel waved back.

"Well, here we go. Thanks for coming with me," Gabriel said as he focused on the road.

Tabitha put her hand on his leg. "I'm excited. I can't wait to see where you grew up."

The young couple drove through the night, trading off every few hours so the other could sleep. The hours on Highway 70 felt long. The scenery was the same . . . fields and more fields. It was miles and miles of flat.

"We should be getting close, only another half an hour or so," Gabriel said as he munched on some jerky.

"There are some really beautiful areas here," Tabitha observed as she watched out the window. "I love the old windmills. It's just so open."

"Yeah. I think that's why I couldn't believe my eyes when I got to the Rockies, ya know? It's so much more wild and extreme."

"Wild and extreme is awesome, but it's nice to have a peaceful break and see something different now and then."

"We'll pass the Cairo Diner on the way to the farm. Mom should be starting her dinner shift. We can surprise her. They have a great meat and three too."

"Meat and three?"

"Yeah, meat and three sides. You've never heard of that?"

"Nope."

"Welcome to Kansas!"

Gabriel was excited to show Tabitha around, but he was nervous for the meeting of the two most important women in his life.

They pulled into the sleepy little town around four thirty in the afternoon. With their windows down, the warm air blew through the cab of the truck. Gabriel saw a few overall-clad farmers chatting outside the filling station, and somebody inside the old hardware shop on the left just flipped the sign to "closed."

"There's the five-and-dime where I used to work." Gabriel pointed across her to the store on the corner. "That's where Jimmy called me to invite me to The River. One of the best days of my life was telling Mr. Baggers, my boss, I was done."

Gabriel rested his forearms on the large steering wheel as he took in the sights. They came to a four-way stop, and Gabriel saw it.

"There it is. I had many a meal at that diner."

He turned into the parking area around the back so his mom wouldn't see him.

"Yep. There's Mom's truck." He slammed the column

shifter into park and turned the engine off. He took a deep breath, exhaled, and leaned back on the old bench seat.

"Does it feel weird?" Tabitha asked as she put on her sandals.

"A little. Just coming back here after all that I've experienced over the past year. It's like I've lived two lifetimes. I spent the bulk of my years here, but at least for now, it just feels strange."

"You know what I'm feeling?" Tabitha asked as she fluffed her hair in the rearview mirror.

"What?"

"I'm feeling like . . . I gotta pee."

"Nice. After you're done, why don't you get us a table and I'll sneak in shortly."

"Got it." Tabitha hoisted herself out of the truck and walked around to the front of the old cinderblock building. Gabriel parked the truck and watched through the window as some of the locals having pie at the counter stared at Tabitha. Her fitted cutoff jeans, tie-dyed tank top, and faded orange dew-rag gave away that she was definitely not from around there.

"May I have a table for two please?"

Gabriel watched as his mom came into view.

"Absolutely, sweetie. Follow me." The waitress took her to a booth in the back of the diner next to a window and slapped a couple of menus down.

"What can I get you to drink?"

"Water, and I'll have some black coffee too." Gabriel saw Tabitha's eyes land on the name tag on the waitress's white blouse. *Maggie.* Tabitha grinned.

Gabriel listened through the open window.

"May I use the restroom?"

"Sure, hon. It's back there . . . the first door on the left." Maggie pointed.

"Thank you." Tabitha headed back.

Maggie headed up to the front to get the drinks. "George. Get your eyes back on your dessert." The sassy waitress obviously caught the old farmer watching the brown-skinned, long-legged beauty as she sashayed to the back of the diner.

The old man choked on his coffee as he spun his barstool back around. His friend next to him slapped him on the arm, and they both got a chuckle.

Gabriel's heart skipped a beat as he peeked through the window and watched his mom head back into the kitchen. He snuck in the front door and joined Tabitha in the booth, facing away from the kitchen.

Maggie came through the swinging door in the back and loaded her tray with two glasses of water. As she was pouring a cup of coffee, the other waitress on duty, a rotund and frumpy dark-haired woman, talked under her breath while looking Tabitha and Gabriel's way.

The couple overheard the comical conversation.

"Did you see that amazing piece of man that just joined little Trixie back there?"

"Oh please, Jenny."

"I'm serious . . . I just saw six feet of a bearded mountain man who is begging for this Kansas girl. Can I take the table, please? I'm going to give that skinny little runway model a run for her money."

Maggie started laughing. "No, I need the tips. Now wipe your chin and get back to work." Maggie headed down the aisle toward Tabitha.

Gabriel kept his head down and looked away as she approached.

"Here you go." She placed the waters and the coffee down. "Would you like to hear the specials?"

"Any chance you have any of Maggie's famous chocolate chip pancakes?" Gabriel looked up at her.

Maggie dropped the empty tray and covered her mouth with both hands.

"Happy birthday, Mom." Gabriel jumped up out of his seat.

"Oh my gosh! I can't believe you!" She hugged his neck.

Gabriel grinned. "Are you surprised?"

"Are you kidding? I'm in shock! Let me look at you!" Maggie grabbed his chin. "What's this? A beard? It's so good to see you. Oh I just can't believe this." She turned her attention to Tabitha, who was smiling from ear to ear.

"You must be Tabitha."

"It's such an honor to meet you." Tabitha extended her arms for a hug.

"Well, I know Gabriel thinks the world of you. She *is* beautiful, Gabriel."

Gabriel winked at Tabitha. "I told you."

Looking at his mom, he added, "I hope Ms. Vonda and Mister Earl don't mind the surprise. I'm assuming we can stay a couple of days at the farm."

"They will be thrilled to see you. It's not the same around the farm without you."

The other waitress came over to the table. "So, Maggie, you know these folks?"

"Jenny, this is my son, Gabriel, and his girlfriend, Tabitha. Jenny has only been here about six months."

The waitress looked Gabriel up and down.

"Well, nice to meet you." She looked at Maggie and pointed her finger up at her. "Don't you say a word."

Maggie motioned to zip her smiling lips. "Not a word."

Jenny smiled. "I'll cover your tables tonight. You go be with your family. I'll even give you the tips! I didn't know it was your birthday!"

"Really? Oh, Jenny, I owe you." Maggie untied her apron as fast as she could.

"Go on before I change my mind!" Jenny shooed them out with both hands.

Gabriel and Tabitha took Gabriel's truck, following Maggie in hers, as they both headed through town to the Cartwright farm. They turned off the main highway onto the first of two unpaved roads. The trucks stirred up a cloud of dust as they motored through the infinite fields. They made the final turn through the gate of the Cartwright Farm. The tires crunched along the gravel drive.

"There's Mister Earl! Hey, Mister Earl!" Gabriel shouted out his window to the old man who was walking out of the barn. The old man squinted and furrowed his brow. The two trucks parked and Gabriel jumped out.

"Holy smokes!" Mister Earl took his John Deere hat off and grinned from ear to ear. Gabriel raced over to the slight man and gave him a big hug. "Where did you come from?"

"I wanted to surprise Mom for her birthday."

Tabitha got out and walked over.

"And who is this pretty little lady?" He extended his wiry arm for a handshake.

"Mister Earl, this is Tabitha. I work with her family at The River in Colorado."

Tabitha flashed a winning smile. "I've heard so much about you, Mister Earl. It's so nice to meet you. Your farm is beautiful!"

He ducked his head. "Oh, it ain't much, but it has served us well. Come on in and see Ms. Vonda. You hungry? You know she'll want to feed you."

"We are starved," Gabriel said. "We'd planned to eat a meat and three, but when Jenny volunteered to take Mom's shift, we ran out of there."

They all ascended the steps of the porch and through the screen door to find Ms. Vonda in her apron bustling around the kitchen.

"Oh my!" The little white-haired woman wiped her hands on her apron as she waddled over to Gabriel and threw her arms up for a hug.

"It's the best birthday present ever!" Maggie said as she watched Ms. Vonda's reaction.

"Fried chicken and biscuits okay for dinner?" She knew how much Gabriel loved her cooking.

"I was hoping you'd say that. Ms. Vonda, this is Tabitha."

"My stars, she's a looker. Are you taking care of my Gabriel? And look how skinny you are. We've got to get some food in you. It's good to meet you, sweetie."

Gabriel laughed to himself. Ms. Vonda only chattered like this when she was nervous or excited.

That night they enjoyed a fantastic Southern meal complete with fried chicken, biscuits, green beans, and sliced tomatoes. Ms. Vonda made Maggie's favorite birthday cake, chocolate with fudge icing. They sat around the dining room table for hours, reminiscing about days gone by on the farm. Maggie asked lots of questions, and Gabriel told of his exploits and discoveries on The River.

For Gabriel, bringing Tabitha to his other home and into his childhood memories was like bringing water to a desert. It felt like healing. She was really getting to know him now. He couldn't wait to show her around. There were new memories to be made on this old property . . . memories that would last a lifetime.

19

The Tractor and the Rain

7:30 a.m. at the Cartwright's Farm

Gabriel woke up to the smell of bacon frying. He'd slept on the sofa in the living room. He heard the guest bedroom door open and Tabitha's feet shuffling into the kitchen where his mom and Ms. Vonda were. He started to get up, but smiled lazily and listened to their conversation instead.

"Did you sleep okay?" Maggie asked.

"Oh yes. I think there's something special about that back room. I don't remember waking up once," Tabitha said, a yawn cutting her short.

"How about some eggs and bacon?" Ms. Vonda asked.

"That sounds wonderful. Can I do anything to help?"

"No, just relax and I'll have you a plate in a jiffy. Coffee or tea?"

"Oh, it feels like a tea kind of day."

Gabriel peeked over the couch to see Tabitha sit down and fold one leg up on the seat under the other.

"A girl after my own heart," his mom said as she took a sip and smiled.

"He's still snoozing away." Ms. Vonda smiled as she placed a full plate of scrambled eggs, bacon, and a blueberry muffin in front of Tabitha.

"I have to say, you sure have had quite an effect on Gabriel. He seems like a part of him just woke up or something." Maggie poured herself a little more hot water as she continued. "We had a pretty rough few years there. I couldn't get him to talk or play with the other boys. He was just a shell. It was really hard, ya know? He just wanted his daddy." Maggie's eyes welled up. "But you seem to have broken through. I can see the way he looks at you. He really loves you."

"I just knew there was something special about him from the first time we met. He seemed to have a deep well in his heart . . . like he was capable of pure greatness. I don't know how to describe it. He was so awkward the first time we talked, but I thought it was cute. I think The River was in him all along. You should see him out there when he's guiding. He has such good instincts and confidence now. I've seen his courage in really difficult situations. It's just amazing to watch. You did a really good job raising him."

Gabriel's heart felt like it was swelling with love for the two women in his life.

"I sure didn't feel like I did at the time. Getting inside the head of a young man isn't the easiest thing. His dad was like that, so inside his thoughts all the time. We made due, though. I had a lot of help." Maggie looked at Ms. Vonda as she cleared some dishes.

"I didn't know he struggled so much as a child."

"He was afraid of his own shadow . . . angry too. He didn't want to have anything to do with the water. He was terrified of it. Thank God for Mister Earl who took him to catch his first fish. All along the way, Gabriel had people in his life, pointing him ahead, helping him on to his destiny. It's beautiful to see him really living . . . to see him so happy. I couldn't give him that."

Tabitha looked thoughtful. "I don't think anyone could give him that. He has to choose it, like the rest of us."

"What do you mean?"

"I think at the end of the day, everyone has to make the choices for their life. As much as I would want to be the source of someone's happiness, I just think that's got to come from something greater. That's too much pressure. We all have to own our decisions for the future and how we are going to live. We can't control life, but we can control how we respond."

"Those are wise words for such a young woman."

"I had a wise mother," Tabitha said humbly. "This breakfast was delicious! Thank you so much. I wish I could cook like that."

"You're quite welcome, darling." Ms. Vonda leaned down in Maggie's ear and whispered loudly, "She's a keeper."

Tabitha excused herself to go get dressed.

Gabriel figured he should have been annoyed that his mom and girlfriend were chatting about his life, but he wasn't. Instead, he just felt loved.

Gabriel sat back on the tractor in the old barn that morning. The smell of hay and rich soil that was caked on the plow filled the air. It was almost time to plant the corn. The sunrays beamed through the cracks in the wood-slatted walls. He loved the sight of all the old tools hanging on the rustic boards. After taking a bite of one of Ms. Vonda's biscuits, he opened The Journal and couldn't believe the entry he found.

> I don't tell her enough, but Helen is my best friend. I married my best friend. She is kind and patient. She is strong and humble. She is ravishing and pure. She has given her life to me all these years. She knows me and I know her. I think the best thing is, we haven't been busy trying to change each other. We share something so deep I can't explain it. If there's one thing I've learned, it's that giving my life to her was the best decision I could have ever made. When you focus on meeting the other's needs, it just all works out. We have walked through the darkest of times and the brightest of days, and we've done it all together. Oh, what majestic mystery in the two becoming one! We have laughed and cried, been at odds and at peace, but never once have we walked it alone. I pray when we go, we go together. I can't imagine life without my Helen. If you find a soul mate, give your life to her or him. Hold nothing back. Never quit. Be quick to forgive. Use soft words. Let the other just be who they were made

to be and cheer your lover on! That's what we learned to do. If you find what I've found, you'll be the luckiest person alive too.

—R. Allen Clarke

1948

The barn door creaked open and startled him.

"There you are," Tabitha said as she let herself in the barn.

Gabriel thrilled at the sight of her. "Hey. Did you have a good sleep?"

"Probably the best sleep I've had in a while. There's just something about that old bed and those quilts. I slept like a baby."

Tabitha walked up and put her hand on his calf.

"Do you know how to drive this thing?"

"Absolutely. Want me to teach you?"

"Are you sure?"

"Climb up."

Gabriel extended his hand and helped her scale the side of the tractor. She plopped down on his lap.

"What does this do?" She started jostling the gearshifts.

"Easy there." Gabriel put his hand on hers. "Let me get us out of here in one piece," he said as he laughed.

He turned the key and started the old John Deere. It chugged and coughed dark smoke into the musty barn air.

"I guess it would help if we opened the doors. Don't touch anything. I'll be right back."

Gabriel jumped down and swung open the massive doors, then climbed back up.

"You ready?" he asked over the rumble of the engine. He locked it into gear and released the clutch. The tractor heaved forward and out into the morning light.

"Woo-hoo! Ride 'em, cowboy!" Tabitha yelled as she held on to the side of Gabriel's legs. He pulled up her hands and placed them on the steering wheel.

"You steer. No sharp turns, okay? Let's head out this way." Gabriel pointed to the large plowed field on the back of the property. He opened up the throttle and the tractor took off.

"Yee-haw!" Tabitha yelled and laughed as they cruised in the wide-open space. "I want one of these!"

The warm wind invigorated Gabriel's face as he felt the pure joy in that moment. They felt no pressing obligations, no heavy sadness, and no worries. They were free.

Gabriel directed her through the fields and down the way to the pond he went to as a young boy. They pulled the tractor up under the giant cottonwood tree he climbed as a youngster. He told her the stories of wrestling matches and fishing. He laughed as he reminisced about the legendary stories of his childhood friends, Jimmy Bly, the gum stealer, General J.J., the giant wrestling champion who ate everything in site, and all the rascals who used to spend their afternoons there.

Gabriel stood up on the tractor seat.

"How's your leg feeling?" he asked her.

"Just fine. Why?"

He clasped his hands to make a step for her.

"You want me to go up there?"

"Yep."

Without hesitation Tabitha stood up, put her hands on his shoulders, and stepped in his hands. He hoisted her, and she grabbed a large branch of the sprawling tree and pulled herself up. Gabriel joined her, and they climbed up a good thirty feet and out on a large branch over the pond.

The two young lovebirds dangled their legs in the breeze as they sat high above the fields of Cairo and shared childhood memories.

"I fell from this very place about ten years ago. Everyone saw it. I was so embarrassed. I fell right on top of this kid Henry. I thought he drowned. I didn't come back to the pond for years." Gabriel squinted as he looked out across the vast landscape. "It feels pretty good to be up here with you . . . and to not be afraid anymore."

"Funny how life works sometimes," she said.

"Yeah."

"The very thing you were terrified of, the weakest part of you, has been turned into the greatest strength. The water was a place of pain and embarrassment, and now it's a place of purpose and passion. You are now helping people overcome their fear and experience The River. How beautiful is that?" Tabitha said.

"You should write this stuff down," Gabriel said as he looked out over the terrain.

"Shut up."

"No, I'm serious. You have a way with words," he said.

Tabitha blushed at his compliment.

"Hey, look over there. We better head back." Gabriel pointed to the dark clouds rolling in from the south. "We get some pretty good storms around here."

They carefully descended the massive tree and hopped back on the tractor. Gabriel fired it up and they drove back toward the farm. Tabitha sat in his lap as they loped down the back road and into the Cartwright field. Thunder started to growl as the cloud cover blocked out the noonday sun. They had a good fifteen minutes to go.

"Uh-oh," Gabriel announced.

Large drops started to fall. The drops sped up quickly into a full downpour. Gabriel slowed the tractor down to a stop.

"What are you doing?" she asked as she peeled the wet hair back from her face.

"Enjoying it!"

Gabriel jumped off the tractor in the middle of the field and started running around holding his arms out and pointing his face to the sky. "Yahoo! Isn't this great!" Tabitha followed suit as the deluge continued. The rain soaked Gabriel to the bone as he drank in the moment.

The rain slowed as the wind coaxed the clouds north. They pulled the clinging shirts away from their bodies, shook the water off their hands, and laughed at how each other looked. Gabriel pulled a piece of wet hair off of her cheek. "You sure are making Kansas a lot more fun." His wide hands cradled her wet cheeks as he leaned down and kissed her on the mouth. The sun appeared from behind the clouds again and warmed Gabriel's skin. They boarded the tractor and headed back to the barn.

"How long can you stay?" Maggie asked as they dug into ham-and-cheese sandwiches, Ms. Vonda's homemade potato salad, Southern sweet tea, and sweet pickles.

Gabriel looked at Tabitha. "I think we'll need to head out tomorrow afternoon at the latest."

His mom looked disappointed. "So soon? You just got here."

"I know, but we have a lot to do to get the camp ready for the season. Why don't you come visit me at The River?"

Maggie got fidgety. "Oh, that's a long ways, and besides, I don't think I could take that much time off of work."

"Well, we need to work it out."

Tabitha chimed in. "We have plenty of room. I'd love for you to see Gabriel in his element."

Maggie got up abruptly and left her napkin on the table. "Please excuse me," she said as she walked back through the hallway to her room.

Mister Earl got up and walked out the door without saying a word.

Ms. Vonda started to clean up.

"You done with that, dear?" She took Tabitha's plate.

Tabitha leaned over to Gabriel. "Was it something I said?" she asked softly.

Gabriel swallowed hard. "It's okay. A lot happened at The River that she probably hasn't faced yet. Corley Falls is home to some hard times for our family. I know all about that. She'll come around."

The next day after lunch, Tabitha and Gabriel packed up the truck and got ready to head out. Another thundershower was on its way as they all gathered around the truck.

Ms. Vonda handed them a basket.

"It's got enough in it to get you home. Plenty of biscuits, Gabriel." The round old lady with her silver hair bun and permanent apron stepped in to give Gabriel a hug. "You take good care of him. I know you will," she said as she hugged Tabitha.

"Great to see you doing so well, son." Mister Earl extended his weathered hand.

Gabriel grabbed hold. "Thank you for everything, Mister Earl."

"I love you." Maggie wiped her eyes as she stood on her tiptoes to give her son a hug. "Be careful, would you?"

Gabriel gave her a warm smile. "I love you too, Mom. I'll call you soon."

Maggie gave Tabitha a hug, then looked into her eyes as she held her shoulders.

"I'm really glad Gabriel has you. You're good for him. You two have something special."

Tabitha met Gabriel's eyes, then said, "It was so good to be with you. Thank you for such an amazing welcome."

Tabitha and Gabriel pulled out onto the long gravel drive and started the long journey home. They waved their hands out the window and watched the three loved ones get smaller and smaller in the rearview mirror.

A few hours into the trip on Highway 70 West, Tabitha broke up the long period of silence.

"So, you know how you said I should write my words down? I wrote something down. Can I read it to you?"

"Yes, absolutely," Gabriel said, pleasantly surprised.

"Don't laugh."

"I wouldn't laugh. Please share."
Tabitha tucked her hair behind her ear as she read.

I saw a beautiful field today, where crops once grew. The earth was broken up and plowed, now ready for seeds to be planted. When the ground is plowed, it loosens those treacherous roots that might choke out the new plants. When the dirt is turned, it allows the soil to absorb the waters from the heavens, and the nutrients from the air. The terrain must be broken for new life to begin. In the rich soil of our lives, there is a season for brokenness—a softening, a turning of the dirt. The rivers and light from the heavens pour down, bringing everything a young seedling needs to flourish and release bounty into the world. As painful as it is, we must let the plow of suffering do its work, for from the broken soil comes a new beginning.

"That's really . . . truly beautiful."
Tabitha laid down on the bench seat in the old truck and rested her head on Gabriel's leg as he drove into the warm Kansas night.

20

Cutthroat & Rainbow

October 5, 2012, 9:30 a.m.

I dozed off just as the sun made its first appearance. The adrenaline from the night on The River had my thoughts and emotions reeling. There's something about physically and psychologically getting out of what's familiar and comfortable. It shakes you out of the hypnotic drone of life's proverbial gerbil wheel. You can get numb and used to hearing the squeak of that wheel go around and around. You chase and chase and chase, and never get there. You want so badly for something to fill you up so you can rest. It's all a mirage. There's no end to it. When you arrive at what you think is the oasis, the pool in the desert, just as you dip your face to drink, it disappears and you get a mouthful of sand. Not this time for me, though. Thanks to

Gabriel and The River, I was off that wheel, and the world was coming alive again.

It felt like I'd only been asleep for five minutes when he stormed through the cabin door to my room.

"You ready?"

It sounded like he was shouting. I jumped out of my skin.

"What?" I said as I sat straight up.

"Let's go catch some dinner!"

"I barely slept." I flopped back down onto the firm bunk mattress.

"You can sleep when you get home, Manhattan." He'd started calling me that on The River the night before. "You ever caught a cutthroat or rainbow?"

"A what? No," I said as I lay there, eyes closed.

"Today's your lucky day, Manhattan! See you at the Jeep in ten." The legendary adventure guide let the spring-loaded screen door slam as he exited.

I looked at the clock and realized I'd actually gotten four hours or so. I put my head in the sink and let the icy mountain water chill my scalp and shock my system awake.

———◆———

The canyon warmed slowly as we approached the edge of the sixty foot drop-off down to The River.

"That's where we are going." Gabriel pointed down to the water's edge.

"How're we getting down there?"

He held up some mountain climbing rope and smiled. This guy had to be over sixty. Unbelievable.

"You're kidding, right?"

"Why would I be kidding? It's way more fun this way."

Once again, way out of my comfort zone.

Gabriel rigged me up with the body harness, belays, and such.

"Here. You'll need these." He handed me some gloves. He gave me strict instructions on how to lean out backward, perpendicular to the cliff, trusting the rope and him to anchor me. I was terrified, but I was determined not to show it.

"Okay, nice and easy," he said confidently.

My fingers gripped the rope so hard they were cramping. I scooted to the edge of the sheer cliff, my heels over the edge. My head started to spin as my heart rate accelerated. He could probably see the terror in my face.

"It's okay. Just lean back. This rope would hold fifty of you."

I took a deep breath and tried to calm down. I didn't realize I could be this afraid.

"Isn't there another way?" I asked through a nervous smile.

"It's not about another way; it's about taking the best way. Enjoy it. You can't get this view, this sensation from walking. Now let's go. Just sit back into the harness."

I obeyed and found myself suspended out over the air, nothing but a canvas harness and a small blue rope keeping me from plummeting to my demise. But once I realized I wasn't going to fall, it was exhilarating. I repelled down to the banks of The River and Gabriel followed. With a large backpack and fly-fishing rods on his back, he raced down the side of the cliff like an army ranger.

"Ha-ha! See what I mean!"

I gave him a high-five.

"Okay, you're right. That was awesome." For a few brief moments I was thinking of something other than my failure.

"Here, this will be yours." He handed me one of the fly-fishing rods. It was much lighter than I expected. We shed the mountain gear, draped the waders over our shoulders, and headed about one hundred yards downstream. All I could hear was the soothing sound of The River bubbling, pouring, and swishing its way through the earth. The waters shimmered in the brilliant sunlight. The giant spruce and fir trees that lined the banks seemed so small next to the mighty granite walls, a far cry from the life I'd known.

"Go ahead and climb in your waders, and we'll get to it," the guide told me.

I tightened the suspenders that held up the rubbery waders.

"I feel like a clown in these things."

"You don't have to wear them. But I'm not sure anyone is looking at your style out here, Manhattan. If you stood in that water for five minutes, you'd be begging me for them."

"Can't we just cast from the shore?"

He walked by me, shaking his head. He turned and started walking backward. "If you fish with me, you have to be in The River. You have to feel the water. Besides, where these fish are, you can't get to them unless you're willing to wade. But, hey, I'll do it my way and you do it yours, and we'll see who comes up with more fish!" The adventurer erupted into a sinister laugh that bounced off the canyon walls.

"I was just asking," I said as I followed him. He kept chuckling.

He showed me the motion of the fly-fishing cast and how it was all about timing and rhythm. He spoke of the art of deceiving the trout with an artificial fly. After about an hour of casting and not catching a single fish, I started to get impatient.

"What am I doing wrong?"

"Just be patient. Your cast looks good," he told me. "See that little eddy on the other side? In front of that rock?" He pointed. "Try and drop her like a feather right in there."

"You already have three fish. I've got to catch up. I don't like being last."

He didn't respond at first. Then after a few casts, he said some things that haven't left me. He sat down on the bank behind me and started attaching a new fly to his line.

"'Many go fishing all their lives without knowing that it is not the fish they are after.' That's Thoreau. Man, he had a way with words. In life, we sometimes fixate on the things that are peripheral to really living. Even out here, you can be so worried about the fish that you miss the sparkling water, the canyon, the peace, and tranquility, the slow-moving clouds and the transcendent beauty all around. By the way, competition is rooted in comparison. In games that's fine. In relationships . . . in life . . . it can be dangerous. You know what I always say? Comparison is the thief of joy. We all have a race to run. That's why I love what old President Hoover said. 'To go fishing is the chance to wash one's soul with pure air, with the rush of the brook, or with the shimmer of sun on blue water. It brings meekness and inspiration from the decency of nature, charity toward tackle-makers, patience toward fish, a mockery of profits and egos, a quieting of hate, a rejoicing that you do not have to decide a darned thing until next week. And it is discipline in the equality of men— for all men are equal before fish.'"

I reeled in my line and pondered what he said.

"Let me see that. I just want to make sure it works." He waded out and took my rod.

Back and forth he slung the tiny fly. The line whipped through the air in a perfect figure eight. He released it and it landed directly in the spot he showed me earlier. Within two seconds his rod bent over. He heaved the rod up, setting the hook.

"There she is!"

He reeled in the most beautiful creature, a rainbow trout.

"That's amazing! How did you do that?"

He grinned slyly. "River secret."

"I'd appreciate it if you'd share it."

"You really want to know?"

He sloshed toward me and handed the rod back to me.

"Luck." We both started laughing. "Try again. Be patient. You'll get one," he said.

I waded back out to the precise spot he was standing. The current pushed gently on my legs. I looked up into the canyon walls and took in the spectacular views. My soul was finally starting to feel the freshness and freedom of the place I was in.

"Here goes," I said as I began to move my forearm. *Ten o'clock—Two o'clock, Ten o'clock—Two o'clock.* I remembered the positions he told me. Then I cast the fly. It lit on the water just downstream of a boulder that created the small eddy.

Then it happened. I felt the jolt as the tip of my rod went down. I yanked it up and started reeling.

"Hey, there you go!" he shouted. "Look at that rod . . . That must be a whale!"

He waded back out to me as I reeled in my very first fish on a fly rod. He brought the net up under it gently.

"Look at that beautiful little cutthroat!"

The fish was only twelve inches long, but I was elated.

He reached in and cradled the fish at the surface of the water so I could get a good look. I had no idea something so small . . . so simple . . . could bring me such joy. He spoke reverently as he used some pliers to remove the hook.

"You always want your hands to be wet when you handle the fish; you don't want the oils to rub off on their scales or gills. It could be deadly to them. Just handle them as little as possible and let them go back to spawn another day," he said as he cradled the trout facing the current until it gradually gained the strength and swam away.

"Wow. What an experience. I get it. I get it," I told him.

He put his hand on my shoulder.

"The River holds many treasures, Blake. Listen to what the waters are saying."

We sat down and enjoyed the delicious ham sandwiches he had prepared for us, and then we packed up our things and started to head out.

"How are we getting out of here?" I asked, thinking about the sheer cliff we repelled down.

"That trail." He pointed downstream.

"Ah. So we didn't *have* to take the terrifying way down."

"You loved it."

"You're right. Are you always right?"

"Just when it matters."

I snickered. "Okay, that was good."

We made a little more small talk as we started to ascend the trail that would lead us back up to the road where we could double back to the Jeep.

"Be careful here. The shale likes to give way," he instructed.

We made several large steps as the trail rose sharply. He stopped in front of me at a small plateau behind a large boulder. I was breathing heavily. He wasn't.

He pointed beneath the rock.

"That's where Rio found Millie."

In an instant I flashed to the storyline of Billy Fielding and the loss of his little girl, and my gut felt hollow. I wondered what kind of a person I'd be if I lost my little girl. We leaned up against the rock wall in silence for at least a minute. Then Gabriel spoke.

"We all have had stuff, stuff in our past buried in the canyon of our lives. Things we've done, or that someone has done to us. When those bones are dug up, pain, grief, and shame . . . man, it all comes crashing in. We feel as small and unworthy as a worm under the dirt. The bones *must* come up. Truth must prevail. That way, they can have a proper burial, and we can move on to new beginnings."

I had no response, just thoughts. His words burrowed deep into my soul. That canyon he was describing that was my life. It felt like the digging began . . . it began when the love of my life discovered I was a cheat, a fraud, and a liar. I wasn't sure there was a new beginning for me. If it was true, I was ready for the bones to come up, whatever it took.

After a few more moments of silence, he said, "I've got one more place I want to take you, and then we'll head back."

21

The Question and the Promise

April 22, 1974

A couple of days after they returned from their visit to Kansas, Gabriel went to The River in the late afternoon before dinner to be alone, just the waters and his thoughts. He rested on a mossy rock that jutted out into the current as he often did. He listened as the water reminded him of his purpose. He felt peaceful rest in these moments. He meditated on the words he'd been reading in The Journal. He spoke often of The River having a voice, and how he loved to hear the waters speak. Gabriel felt the truest version of himself when he was at The River. It was a beautiful trip to Kansas to see his mom, to see where he spent most of his early years, but The River was home now. Gabriel took time that warm afternoon to contribute to The Journal.

Thank you for bringing me home. I don't understand how everything works. I know I've been fortunate. My life is rich. I have a purpose. I'm learning now, I'm not owed anything. I'm just grateful. It's not about what you think you should've gotten in life; it's about living every moment grateful for each day, each breath, each pulse of the heart, each person in your life. Nothing is guaranteed. I want to make the most of every day. Today I decide, today I choose, today I can give myself away and live a life of love . . . a life that speaks of destiny. I want to make memories that last forever!

The spring sun lifted the canyon temperatures into the eighties. Gabriel took off his river sandals, rolled his pants up, and slipped his feet into the chilly waters, wiggling his toes. The sun's rays warmed his cheeks. A familiar screech radiated from the sky. He peeked through a squint to see the silhouette of a majestic hawk passing back and forth in front of the sun. A smile emerged while he remembered his first night back at The River. The stirring of the waters, his first encounter with Tabitha, and his first run on the big white water, all vivid memories of how he wrestled with his grief in the gentle arms of The River. On the cusp of drifting off to sleep, he caught a whiff of a familiar smell, vanilla tobacco smoke. He opened his eyes to see the white-haired black man crouched over him with a puzzled brow and his pipe clinched in his teeth.

Gabriel started.

"Ezra!"

"I wasn't sure if you were breathin'!"

"You gotta warn me next time." Gabriel laughed as he sat up.

Ezra grunted as he lowered himself slowly and sat down next to him.

"I was just out for a walk and here's this lifeless body layin' on a rock. Dear Lord." The old man started the deep and raspy cough that had been plaguing him through the winter.

"Are you feeling okay, Ezra?"

The coughing fit kept up a little longer.

Gabriel frowned. "You need to get to a doctor."

"I'll be fine, son."

"I need you around, you know. I'm going to do something, Ezra . . . something big." Gabriel smiled as he looked out over the sun-drenched white water.

"Oh really?" Ezra puffed more smoke into the air as Gabriel tried to find the words.

Gabriel continued, "When you know you're supposed to be with someone, you know it in your soul, and I know . . . I just want to spend the rest of my life with her. That's all there is to it."

Ezra's face lit up. "Oh, sweet cinnamon. Are you gonna . . . ?"

Gabriel nodded.

Ezra wore a look of pure contentment as he peered out over the water.

"When?"

"Tomorrow night."

"Does Jacob know?"

Gabriel nodded again.

"Oh, my Lord, my Lord. I hoped beyond hope I'd live to see this day."

———◆———

The next day around lunchtime, Gabriel found Tabitha reading out on the deck of the lodge.

"Hey, don't go anywhere tonight. I've got plans for us."

She laid her book on her chest.

"Oh really? What kind of plans?" She grinned.

"Nothing big. Just plans. I'll meet you right here at seven o'clock."

She flashed a brilliant smile. "Okay, then."

Gabriel tried to hold his excitement back. "Seven o'clock." He pointed at her.

She pointed back and touched her finger to his.

"Seven o'clock, Mr. Clarke."

———◆———

The night was warm and clear. Gabriel wore his favorite thin denim shirt and faded Levi blue jeans. He sat in his old step-side pickup, waiting for Tabitha to appear from the lodge. His heart raced as he thought of all the things that could go wrong. He wanted it to be perfect. He had cleaned out his truck earlier in the day, but he noticed a new place where the cloth bench seat split again.

"Agh!"

He yanked the duct tape from his glove box and peeled the tape off. He put it up to his mouth to rip it with his teeth. Just then, he looked up and saw her. He froze. He'd never seen her like this. He'd never seen anyone or anything more beautiful. Standing on the steps in a faded chambray cotton sundress, Tabitha looked radiant. She had a white sweater draped over her arm, her dark auburn hair poured down past her bare shoulders, and her green eyes seemed almost translucent. She made her way down the steps in her worn leather sandals. Her beauty seemed effortless. She pushed her hair behind one ear and smiled at Gabriel. He leaned down as he ripped the tape and slapped it on the seat, hoping she didn't see him. He threw the tape under the seat and opened his door to get out and greet her. In his haste, he caught his boot between the door and the floorboard and fell out flat on his stomach in the gravel drive. Before Tabitha could say anything, he jumped up to his feet.

"I'm okay! I'm okay!" His face felt red hot.

"Oh my gosh! Are you sure?" Tabitha asked through a smile.

"Oh yeah, I'm fine. You know, I meant to do that." He brushed the dirt off his palms and walked her around to the passenger side of the truck.

"Oh, absolutely. I could tell that was staged." They both started laughing.

He opened the door and she climbed in, tucking her dress underneath her.

He shut her door and rested his hands on the open window.

"What I wanted to say before I dove out of the truck a minute ago was, 'Miss Fielding, you look stunning tonight.'"

"Why, thank you, Mr. Clarke. You look quite handsome yourself."

She put her hand on his forearm. It sent shivers up his spine.

"So where are you taking me?"

"You'll see." Gabriel jogged around the front of the truck and got in.

"Wow, so secretive. You've really got me wondering now."

Gabriel tried to play it cool as he pulled out onto the road.

After a half an hour of winding through the canyon into the night, Gabriel pulled off the road and parked the truck. He grabbed a backpack out of the bed of the truck and threw it on his shoulders. After lighting a kerosene lamp and setting it on the hood, he opened her door and offered his hand to her to help her out.

"I'm going to need you to wear this." He held up a folded red bandana.

"What?"

"Just trust me." He started to tie it around her eyes.

She pulled back.

"Why do I need this? It's dark, Gabriel."

"Trust me," he said calmly as he persisted. "That's not too tight, is it?"

"No."

He took her hand and led her down the path into the quiet forest. He pushed away branches and talked her over rocks and holes as the sound of the bubbling waters grew.

"This is The Beach, isn't it?" she asked.

"Uh-huh," Gabriel answered as he guided her out of the

last group of trees and onto the clearing next to The River where they first met. The night sky was crystal clear. The moonlight bounced off the water, and the starlight canopy twinkled like diamonds. Gabriel's heart beat fast.

He wiped his sweaty palms on his pants. "You ready?"

"Yes, of course I'm ready!"

He stood behind her and untied the bandana slowly.

Tabitha gasped and put her hands over her mouth.

All over The Beach, on the rocks that jutted out into the water, and even on some boulders in the middle of The River, sat dozens of candles, flickering in the night. In the middle of the sandy clay, a small fire crackled and a large blanket was spread out next to it. On the blanket were two place settings of dishes and silverware.

"How did you do this?" Her eyes welled as she took it all in.

Gabriel felt like a little boy on Christmas morning. "I have my ways. Dinner is waiting for us. Come join me."

He led her over to the fire and took off his backpack. She knelt down at one of the place settings. He took a towel and some tongs from his bag and pulled the crumpled tin foil from the coals. "Potatoes, mushrooms, and onions, sautéed in butter, just like you like them." He pulled another from underneath the coals and opened it up carefully. The steam of the juicy meat rose into the air. "Rosemary rib eye . . . campfire style." He divided the large steak into two pieces and loaded their plates.

"This is unbelievable. I just don't know what to say."

"You don't have to say anything. Oh! I almost forgot." Gabriel jumped up and went over behind a rock and pulled out a small tin bucket full of ice with bottles of Coca-Cola buried in it. He pulled out two, opened them, and sat down on the blanket.

Taking a deep breath, he asked, "Shall we eat, Miss Fielding?"

Tabitha leaned across their plates of food, grabbed the back of Gabriel's neck, and pulled him in close for a long kiss.

The couple enjoyed their succulent meal in the beauty of the canyon. Their conversation was easy.

"I think it's pretty amazing that we met like we did. I didn't know you were one of *the* Clarkes. I mean, what are the chances, you know?" Tabitha took a sip of her Coca-Cola. "I wasn't even going to go on the trip, but something told me I should just go."

"I'm sure glad you did. You've changed everything for me . . . for the better," Gabriel said. "Now being here with you, it's pretty much all I could ever want. Remember that time Cig was so drunk . . . and Rollie Sever with his unbuttoned shirt and chest of bear fur?"

"Oh, Cig . . . so gross . . . and the bravado of that guy Rollie, and that hair?" Tabitha wrinkled her nose and shook her head.

"Those guys were crazy, but it made for some great memories," Gabriel said as they both laughed hard.

"The River brought us together," Tabitha said as she looked into his eyes.

"To The River." Gabriel raised his Coke bottle, and they toasted their journey together.

Their conversation slowed as they finished the last few

bites. Gabriel stood to his feet and helped Tabitha up. They walked arm in arm over to the water's edge.

They faced each other. Tabitha looked around the canyon and up at the night sky.

"All these candles, it's like we got to eat in the heavens, surrounded by stars."

Gabriel looked down at the ground and then into Tabitha's eyes as he swallowed hard. He felt small beads of sweat form on his temples.

"I have a few things to say to you, Tabitha, so bear with me . . . I'll try to get through it." He took her hands in his.

"Okay," she said tenderly.

"I haven't been able to take my eyes off of you since you stepped out of that van that day . . . right over there." He nodded to the edge of the trees. "Never in a million lives did I think I'd be with a girl as amazing as you. You're beautiful beyond my words to describe. You have made me a better man, a better human. Jimmy invited me to see The River, but you called me to experience it. You got me in . . . all the way in. It's not just with the water either. It's in all of life. You've helped me awaken to real life and shown me there's more. You have been strong when I've been weak. You've lifted me when I couldn't lift myself." Gabriel's eyes welled up as his voice quivered. "I love you, Tabitha."

She didn't blink as she stared at him intensely.

"Come over here." Gabriel led her just a few steps upstream to a small spruce near the edge of The River. As they approached, Gabriel held the lantern up to illuminate the tree. Tabitha noticed the shape of a heart etched deeply into the tree bark. She ran her fingers over it.

"I carved this here that first night I saw you," he said. "I know it's kind of silly. It was just my way of remembering the most amazing night of my life."

Tabitha saw something hanging just above it.

Dangling on a small branch was a braided leather necklace holding a small heirloom diamond ring. She looked at Gabriel and smiled as wide as the canyon.

Gabriel lifted the leather necklace off the tree. "I don't know exactly what the future holds, but I do know this . . . I'm madly and hopelessly in love with you. From my head to my toes, I know that I want to be with you forever. I promise you, if you'll have me, I will love you until I draw my last breath."

He opened the clasp and slid the small vintage-looking silver ring off.

He knelt down and held the ring up to her. It glistened in the moonlight.

"Tabitha Fielding, will you marry me?"

She paused for a second, and his heart pounded in his chest. Then her eyes pooled with tears as she nodded. She laughed and blurted out, "Yes! Yes! A thousand times, yes."

He slid the ring on her finger. She lunged into his arms, tackling him on The Beach. They held each other and laughed through their joyful tears.

"I was meant for you and you for me." Tabitha propped herself up with her elbows on his chest. "How in the world did you make all this happen?"

Gabriel grinned.

"She said yes!" Gabriel shouted as he turned his head back toward the woods.

A cheer erupted, and out of the forest came a group of people hooting and hollering.

Tabitha jumped to her feet, her mouth gaping open as she saw her dad, Sadie, all the guides, and friends she knew around the camp. Jacob walked up to her and picked her up in a tight hug. Ezra stood quietly in the back smiling contentedly like a doting grandpa. Everyone was shouting and clapping. Most of them lit sparklers, some carried coolers of more food and drink, and then some came running and splashed into the water. The joy echoed throughout the canyon.

Samuel approached the couple. Gabriel squeezed Tabitha in close by the waist.

"Congratulations, you guys." Samuel looked at Tabitha, and she smiled nervously. "I wish you guys the best, I really do." Samuel held his hand out to Gabriel. Gabriel shook it firmly.

"Thanks, Samuel."

Samuel turned and walked away to talk with some of the others.

"Hear, hear!"

Jacob got everyone's attention as he raised his drink into the air.

"Here's to one of the most beautiful nights of our lives at Big Water Adventures! To Tabitha and Gabriel and their life together at The River!"

22

Covenant Day

September 17, 1974, 2 p.m.

"From The Journal, 1946, R. Allen Clarke." The white-bearded minister peered through his reading glasses as he read from the leather artifact.

> The two rivers carve their way around and through every mountain and valley to find each other. Nothing can keep them apart. The pursuit is unceasing and unstoppable, and all the while, every insurmountable obstacle is bringing them together. The two waterways swirl into one—each flow is a different color, a different temperature, a different strength, and a different depth—and as the two rivers come together, they form one that is greater, stronger, more diverse, and even more beautiful. Once the waters

mix, they are never the same. They will never go back to
the way they were. The two names become one name, and
this river will flow in unrelenting beauty and power as it
nourishes and shapes the land. The confluence will be far
more than one smaller river could be alone. This river will
display all that's beautiful in nature. So too in this covenant, two lives shall come together as one. These lives are
forever changed. A new beginning is created. Therefore,
what The Great River has put together, nothing on earth
will tear it apart.

The rafting season ended with perfection. On a warm,
September Saturday, dozens of young guides, friends, and
family lined The Beach, facing The River for the life-giving
ceremony.

Tabitha, in a white flower head wreath and long, white
cotton dress, stood barefoot and glowing as she stared into
Gabriel's eyes. To Gabriel, she looked like an angel sent from
the Maker Himself. Sadie stood at her side holding a beautiful
bouquet of fresh wildflowers. Jimmy Bly, the best man, stood
behind Gabriel. The minister from Corley Falls's little white
church up the way, Reverend Bellows, officiated with his back
to the waters. Gabriel felt every moment in his soul. When
he saw Ezra quietly next to Jacob with his Sunday best on, he
thought about all those talks on the porch. Jacob fought tears
as he gave his daughter away. It was Maggie's first trip back
to The River since she came to pick up five-year-old Gabriel
after his father's accident. She seemed to have so many mixed
emotions, but most of all she looked overjoyed as she saw how
happy her son had become. Ms. Vonda held tight to Maggie's

arm, and Mister Earl never stopped grinning as they witnessed Gabriel's new life at The River. Billy watched a few rows back.

Reverend Bellows looked over and nodded at Sadie. She set her flowers down and picked up her ukulele and started to strum. Her lilting angelic voice echoed throughout the canyon with the beautiful melody she composed to a poem Gabriel had written for Tabitha.

Hearts arrested by the glance of souls through fragile eyes
Hope of what could be the journey for our destiny
Angels are dancing here tonight
Heaven descended for me just in time
Light cascading down
Upon your skin now I am found
Love, can this be true
My heart ablaze for only you
Angels are dancing here tonight
Heaven descended for me just in time
Love, could this be true
My heart ablaze for only you
My heart ablaze for only you

Gabriel didn't take his eyes off of Tabitha, but he could hear the sniffles from the guests. Reverend Bellows looked back at the couple.

"Who is giving this woman to be married to this man?"

"I am," Jacob replied tenderly. He stepped forward to kiss Tabitha on the cheek. "I love you, sweetheart. I'm so proud of you," her dad whispered in her ear.

The minister continued.

"Today is a special day . . . a day of new beginnings. What's past is gone . . . it's over, and today you start your new life together. You are giving yourselves to each other in a sacred covenant. This is a mutual submission of the heart. Hold fast to each other. Gabriel, love Tabitha, give your life up for her, even as God in Christ has loved His people and given His life up for us. Tabitha, love Gabriel, and partner with him in every way on this new journey you are on together. May your home be a home marked with every facet of the greatest of all virtues, love. As the Holy Scriptures say, 'Love is patient, love is kind. It does not envy, it does not boast, it is not proud. It does not dishonor others, it is not self-seeking, it is not easily angered, and it keeps no record of wrongs. Love does not delight in evil but rejoices with the truth. It always protects, always trusts, always hopes, always perseveres.' So remember, Gabriel and Tabitha, may love . . . this kind of love, stay at the center of your life together."

Next to the minister sat a small table with two clay pots filled with water and an empty crystal vase. The minister nodded to Gabriel and Tabitha and motioned to the vessels. Gabriel and Tabitha picked up each pot and poured the water into the crystal vase.

"The waters from these clay vessels represent the life of Gabriel and Tabitha individually. Just as the waters are poured into the clear vase, so too their lives are poured together as one. As the light shines through the crystal and into the water, prisms of color beam out. This is a beautiful symbol of their love for one another creating beauty all around them."

The couple returned to their place in the center.

"Gabriel, your vows please."

Gabriel swallowed hard. He couldn't believe he was standing in front of her. He breathed deeply and looked to the sky to gain his composure. His deep voice quivered as he read his vows.

"Tabitha, in our covenant together, I give you my heart. I will protect you, walk with you, comfort you, serve you, and love you always. Wherever our journey leads us, I promise to stay by your side. There is not a shadow of evil or temptation that will steal the light from the candle I hold for you in my heart. Hand in hand, there is nothing we cannot face. You are my best friend and the fulfillment of dreams that only the depths of my heart knew. I promise to be yours and yours alone." Gabriel wiped his eyes with the back of his hand.

"Tabitha, your vows please."

Tabitha smiled brilliantly as she spoke.

"Gabriel, in our covenant together, I give you my heart. You are the man of my dreams. You possess a greatness and humility that make me want to be like you . . . It makes me want to follow your lead. I'll walk with you, comfort you, serve you, and love you always. Wherever The River of life takes us, I'll be in the raft with you. I will hold nothing back from you. You are my best friend and the man I was made for. I promise to be yours and yours alone."

"May I have the rings please?"

Jimmy and Sadie passed the rings to the minister.

"These rings are an unending circle . . . a symbol of your undying devotion one to another. Gabriel, repeat after me. 'With this ring I pledge my unending love for you.'"

Gabriel's quivering hand placed the ring on her finger as he spoke. "With this ring I pledge my unending love for you."

"Tabitha, repeat after me. 'With this ring I pledge my unending love for you.'"

Tabitha held his hand in hers and placed the silver ring on his finger as she responded, "With this ring I pledge my unending love for you."

"Ladies and gentlemen, in front of these witnesses and by the power vested in me by the state of Colorado, I present to you Mr. and Mrs. Gabriel Clarke."

The minister spoke louder over the cheer that erupted. "Gabriel, you may kiss your bride!"

Gabriel cradled her face in his hands and pressed his lips to hers. The onlookers clapped and whistled.

The minister got everyone's attention.

"Gabriel and Tabitha would like each of you to take a river stone from the water's edge, and we will all line up together and cast them into the water. Before we do, they'd like you to each say a prayer for their journey. This gesture is to signify their undying devotion to each other and to The River, no matter where the waters take them."

Everyone lined the shore, the bride and groom in the center, holding the smooth stones.

Amidst everyone shuffling around, Gabriel found himself standing next to Jacob and Billy.

"Great day, huh?" Jacob said as he tossed a rock back and forth between his hands.

Gabriel grinned and Billy nodded.

Jacob continued, "Whenever I do this, I like to look at

these rocks as my past mistakes. Once they plunge in The River, they go away. They turn into something else and I never see them again."

"Not enough rocks in this canyon for me to throw," Billy said, casting a glance at Gabriel.

"For me either." Jacob chuckled.

"It's going to be different for me, Jacob. I suppose I've got quite a few days ahead of me. Might as well live 'em."

Gabriel and Jacob both reached out to sqeeze Billy's shoulders; then Gabriel turned back to his bride.

The minister called out, "As The River has shaped these stones, may it always shape us! One . . . two . . . three!"

"Woo-hoo! Hear! Hear!"

The sound of the stones crashing in the water reverberated as everyone applauded again.

———◦❈◦———

Back at the lodge, the feast was underway. Flickering torches lined the deck, casting light on the storytellers' faces. Outbursts of laughter joined the sounds of the water as it rippled along.

Jimmy Bly stood up and clanked his glass with his fork. The conversational roar quieted quickly. Gabriel looked nervous at what his friend might say.

"Hey, everyone. I wanted to offer a toast to the bride and groom. Gabriel, you're a long way from Kansas, brother. To see you out here, I just know it's where you are meant to be. It's Cairo's loss, though. How you got this girl's attention, I'll never know! Maybe it's 'cause you were with me when you first came to The River!" Everyone howled. "Seriously, you always had a kind word for me, and I'm proud of you. You're like a little brother to me. Even though you're bigger and stronger, you *are* younger. I wish you guys all the happiness in the world. You deserve it. I love ya!"

Glasses clinked musically.

Sadie stood up.

"I guess it's my turn. I'll try not to cry." She looked at Tabitha seated next to her. "I look up to you so much. You are an amazing woman. I couldn't be happier for you. I love you, and I'm so grateful for the way you have looked after me and taught me. When Mom died, you were my rock. I know she is here with us and celebrating you too. Gabriel, you saved my life!" She turned to the group. "He actually kept me from being eaten by a bear! Even before the wedding, you were like a big brother to me. Thank you for taking care of my sis. You are strong and wise, and if you have a little brother hiding anywhere, I'd like to know, please."

"Freddie Clarke here!" Freddie chimed up from the back, and Gabriel nearly fell off his chair from laughing.

After they all had their cake, Gabriel excused himself from the table and headed into the lodge. He headed through the kitchen and saw his mom sitting at the dining table flipping through some pictures.

"Hey, Mom. Are you okay?"

"I'm fine, sweetheart. I'm just remembering. Look at this one. You were eight and you did *not* want me taking your picture. You just looked so cute with the dirt on your face. Here's one at the farmers' market; remember that day? I thought I almost lost you."

"Yeah, I still have the marbles from the magic river man." Gabriel smiled at the memory.

She grabbed his broad shoulders.

"I'm so, so proud of you, Gabe. She's such a wonderful girl." She wiped some icing off his scruffy beard. "Don't forget about me, okay?"

"Mom, I could never forget about you."

"I know, I know. It's just so far."

"I want you to come out here and spend some time with us . . . make some new memories. There are some amazing people out here. I'll take good care of you. I'll save up and help you pay for the trips. Life is too short. You could let me take you down The River."

"Oh really? Okay, we'll see." She smiled warmly. "I love you, honey."

"I love you, Mom."

Gabriel gave his mom a hug and walked back outside onto the deck with her.

She walked away, and Jacob approached.

"So, I guess you're my son-in-law now." The gray curly-headed guide squinted as he looked at Gabriel.

"Yes, sir."

"Take good care of my Tabby, okay?"

"Most definitely, sir."

Jacob pulled him in and hugged him tightly.

"I love you, son. You're home. If you need anything, I'm here."

"Thank you, Jacob. That means the world." Gabriel felt a new sense of belonging at Jacob's words.

"I'll go get things ready for you guys." Jacob walked off the deck and over to the gear shed.

Gabriel felt a hand on his back. He turned to see his faithful and wise friend Ezra. Gabriel's eyes filled with tears at the sight of him.

"So, I guess you married the canyon princess, young man. Not bad. Not bad at all." His raspy laugh was contagious.

"Thank you, Ezra."

"For what?"

"For everything."

"Oh, go on now, you had it all along."

"I'm serious, Ezra. I don't know where I'd be if it weren't for you. You keep me on the right path. You help me think straight."

"Well, I guess we needed each other. I'm proud of you, son. You are on your way."

Gabriel leaned down and hugged him. "I love you, Ezra."

"Alright now. Alright. That's enough," Ezra said as he slapped Gabriel's back.

"It's all ready!" Gabriel heard Freddie's shout from the water's edge.

"I better go." Gabriel rushed inside the lodge. All the family and friends headed down to the water where Tabitha and Gabriel emerged a few minutes later in full river gear. They climbed into a raft with big white letters stenciled on the bow, G & T C L A R K E. To the sound of cheers, Gabriel and Tabitha kissed, then floated off into the moonlit current.

23

Ezra's Journey and the Gift

February 9, 1975, 7:25 p.m.

Gabriel blew into his cupped hands to warm them as he crunched along the icy path at twilight. The clear sky and the brilliant moon caused the water to glow in a soft white. Gabriel took long walks along the water during the winter. The River was quieter during these months as portions of it would ice over, and the blue and gray tones of the canyon carried an eerie stillness. To Gabriel, the waters seemed even more mysterious in the winter. An occasional distant hoot of an owl or haunting bay of a wolf would break into the silence. He and Tabitha had been married for a few months now, living in a small cabin on the north side of the lodge. They would soon depart for the North Camp to begin preparations for running that location in the coming rafting season. Wearing his favorite gray scarf knitted by Ms. Vonda and a weathered black peacoat, the once-timid Kansas farm boy, now rugged river man, headed downstream toward his old cabin room that neighbored Ezra's.

Gabriel ascended the steps to the porch and heard the old man struggling through a violent cough.

"Ezra?" Gabriel opened the screen and leaned in close to the door. "Ezra, are you okay?"

The cough continued.

Gabriel let himself in and quickly grabbed a hand towel by the sink and handed it to the feeble older man as he helped lower him in his wooden rocker. Gabriel went over to the sink, drew a cup of water from the faucet, and handed it to Ezra. The older man seemed significantly weaker since Gabriel had seen him a few days before.

"Jacob will be ready in about thirty minutes or so. Do you need any help with your things?" Gabriel said in a concerned tone.

Ezra's hand shook as he pointed to a small tweed suitcase on the bed.

"I can't get that blasted thing zipped. I don't know why we are doing this. I'll be fine."

"Well, we're all a little worried about you, Ezra, so you are going to get this checked out. We'll get you some medicine and get you back here to work."

Ezra didn't respond. He motioned to a box in the back corner of the room.

"Can you bring that over to me, son?"

Gabriel picked up the square wooden box about the size

of a shoebox and handed it to Ezra. It was covered in burlap and tied together with a thin leather strap.

Ezra held it on his lap.

"I've been meaning to give this to you. It took me longer than I thought. I wanted to have it ready to give you at the wedding but better late than never. I hope you like it." Ezra pushed it out on the edge of his knees.

Gabriel looked stunned.

"Wow, thank you. What is it?"

"Open it."

Gabriel untied the strap and unfolded the burlap material. It revealed a beautifully stained wood box with hinges on the back and a clasp in front. On the top of the box was the symbol, charred into the face of the wood.

"The symbol of Ama-Woya," Gabriel said as he admired the beauty and craftsmanship.

Ezra nodded once. "Open it up."

Gabriel raised the lid of the box, revealing another item wrapped in the same burlap cloth. He looked at Ezra as he picked it up.

"Now read the message." Gabriel noticed the handwritten message on the inside of the box lid. He read aloud.

To my dearest Gabriel and Tabitha,

Please accept the work of my hands as a symbol of how much you mean to me. Remember you are loved and you are never alone. Hold on to each other. Embrace your freedom. Above all, give yourselves away. It's only in giving yourself away that you find your path. May each sunrise be a new beginning. Burn the records of each other's faults. Forgive often. Love well. You both will always be in my heart.

Your friend in The River,
Ezra Buchanan

Gabriel felt a lump growing in his throat.

Ezra nudged him. "Go on, unravel it."

Gabriel removed the shroud, unveiling an extraordinary wood carving of a beautiful Native American woman. Gabriel stared, speechless.

"It's what I thought she must have looked like."

Gabriel paused, lost in admiration. "Ezra, I don't know what to say. This is a masterpiece. The detail, the expression on her face, it's just breathtaking! I had no idea you could do this." Gabriel ran his fingers over the grooves of her hair, and the solitary tear coming out of her deep and mournful eyes. He noticed the broad nose and smooth glow of her cheeks that had been polished into the wood.

"I'm glad you like it," Ezra said through a peaceful smile. "Ama-Woya is a symbol of freedom. She represents shedding the heavy chains that weigh us all down . . . Yep . . . she ran to her destiny, no matter the cost. Scars came along the way, but they just served to remind her what she'd come from, and how much she had to live for."

Gabriel ran his fingers down the face of the wooden sculpture.

"It looks just like her . . . I can't even believe it." Gabriel shook his head as he studied the work of art.

"Looks just like who?"

Gabriel spoke softly as the memories flooded him. "Back

in Kansas in grade school, during one of the darkest times I can remember, a very special woman . . . a teacher . . . came into my life. She was beautiful inside and out. Her love and encouragement got me through. She stood up for me. In fact, she'd lost her father too. Somehow she reached down into my world and pulled me up. This carving is Ama-Woya"—Gabriel pointed at her face emphatically—"but it's also Lily Collingsworth."

"Ah. The teacher who painted The River for you, yes?"

"Yes, her Cherokee name was Aykwa-Aykwanee. It means Great River."

"Hmm." Ezra pursed his mouth and squinted in concentration. "Guess The River never left you, even in Kansas. Look at you now, son." Ezra rocked his chair slowly as he blinked hard and looked out the window. A light snow began to fall.

Ezra continued in a calm and steady tone.

"In the winter, The River gets quiet. Under the ice, we can't see the flow. But you must always remember, the current still moves . . . in ways we can't see. Never fear; just trust that the truth is moving and working its way. You'll know soon enough." Ezra started to cough violently.

"Do you need some water?" Gabriel asked.

Ezra shook his head and continued.

"When spring comes, the ice melts, and The River shows off. She takes all the rocks and boulders we river runners view as obstacles, and splashes around and over, and turns them into beauty. Life will give you obstacles; let the current take you around, over, and through, Gabriel. Remember, what we think are detours just might be destiny."

Gabriel sat on the edge of the bed, holding the gift and listening intensely.

Ezra's words slowed with every sentence as he continued, "You and Tabitha are starting your life at the North Camp soon. Everything will flow from your life together." Ezra raised his tired hands and clasped them together. "Remember, love is laying your life down for her. Jacob tells me you are going to start building a house for the two of you up there. Remember, you are not just building a physical house; you are building a sacred home. Don't let anything tear it apart. She will make mistakes. Let it go. You will make mistakes. Own them. And get on with new beginnings. You're going to do just fine, Gabriel Clarke. You were made for The River."

Gabriel rested his hand on Ezra's forearm and smiled knowingly.

"You always have the right words. I don't say it enough, Ezra. I don't know where I'd be without you. I don't know where to begin. You are like a window, a view into what should be in this life. I treasure every word . . . I hold them close. I want you to know that."

Ezra squeezed Gabriel's hand. Gabriel heard a noise outside, so he got up and looked through the window.

"Here comes Jacob. Looks like it's time for you to go."

Gabriel walked over and helped Ezra up out of his chair.

Ezra grunted. "That used to be a lot easier."

"Don't forget your coat. It's pretty cold out there." Gabriel took it off the rocker and draped it over his shoulders.

"Pass me my hat."

Gabriel grabbed the old, black wool porkpie hat with a small gray feather. Ezra put it on his head.

Jacob opened the door and dusted the snowflakes from his hat and shoulders.

"You about ready, Ezra? It's starting to come down out there. We better get going before the roads cover up. This your bag?"

Ezra nodded as Jacob picked it up. Ezra grabbed his hand-carved cane from the corner.

Gabriel put his own coat back on. "Jacob, will you call me and let me know you guys got in alright?"

"Sure. I'll keep you posted."

Jacob took the small suitcase and headed out to the Jeep. Gabriel walked out with Ezra and gave him a hand getting in. Ezra's cough started up. As Jacob flicked the lights on and started to back out, Gabriel waved his arms to stop him.

He approached Ezra's door and opened it. "I forgot something." Gabriel reached in and wrapped his arms around the old man. "I'll see you soon."

"You better believe it, son. One way or another. In The River . . . always in The River."

"I'll call you," Jacob said as he pushed the clutch in and jammed the gearshift in reverse.

Gabriel stood in the quiet snowfall and waved good-bye. Ezra tipped his hat to the young guide and smiled.

Gabriel made his way back up the steps of the cabin to Ezra's room to close things up. As he approached the small wooden nightstand to switch off the rustic lamp, he noticed an unsealed envelope. On the outside, in a shaky cursive writing, it read, "September of '44." Gabriel pried it open with his thumb and forefinger to find an old picture. He held it under the light. It looked like a young Ezra, standing in The River with a minister and host of people on the banks watching. A baptism. Gabriel stared in amazement at the piece of history, and the words of his faithful friend echoed in his heart: "In The River, always in The River." He laid it back down on the night table and switched off the light.

Gabriel picked up his carving and carefully wrapped it up in the box. He walked across the creaking wood floor and back out into the snow. As he made his way back down the path next to The River, he couldn't help but rehearse his encounter with Ezra that night. He took his time in the biting cold. He thought about how far he'd come, and how far he had to go. He missed Ezra already.

24

Thanksgiving and the News

The Lodge at the North Camp in Corley Falls, Colorado, 1977

A fire crackled and hissed in the large stone hearth at the lodge, a steady warmth against the cold outside. Gabriel, Tabitha, their families, and the guides were buzzing around the kitchen getting the last of the food and condiments in place. A succulent smoked turkey, cranberry-cornbread stuffing, sweet potatoes, and butter beans joined the biscuits and jams on the long reclaimed barn-wood table.

"I think we are ready, guys," Gabriel said loudly, trying to get everyone's attention. "Billy, would you mind lighting the center candle?" Gabriel handed him the box of matches. A large handmade candle sat in the center of the long, plank spruce table surrounded by river stones. The family of guides took their seats around the table and quieted down as Gabriel read aloud from The Journal.

> We give thanks for the rain. We give thanks for the sun. We give thanks for the mountain. We give thanks for the valley. For in the depths, we are shaped and strengthened. We give thanks for the water, how it flows to the lowest places and for the life that it brings. In everything and in every season, we give thanks. May gratitude mark our journey, opening our hands to give, and our hearts to love. We have been given much, and in our plenty, we too will give. For open hands are never empty, and open hearts never alone.

Gabriel closed The Journal slowly. Everyone sat for a moment in silence, as was the tradition. Jacob offered a prayer of thanks.

"Maker, Father of heaven and earth, we humble our hearts to thank You for this moment, for life, and for each other. Our hearts are overwhelmed as we think of those who cannot be with us." He paused. "We are grateful beyond words for all who are with us today. May Your love and forgiveness be found in the current of each life at this table. Move in us. Move through us. Our hands are Your hands. Our feet are Your feet. We come to You in the name of the Son who died for the forgiveness of mankind. Amen."

"Amen," they all chimed in a broken unison.

"Let's dig in, everyone!" Sadie said as she scooped the first bit of stuffing onto her plate. The crescendo of conversation picked back up to a roar as plates were passed and filled.

All the guides sat around a couple of makeshift tables. At the head table, Gabriel sat at one end with his bride of just over three years to his right. Samuel and Sadie on one side, Freddie and Billy sat opposite them next to Tabitha, and Jacob sat at the other end.

Jacob inserted himself into the bustling conversation.

"So, while we're eating, why don't each of us take a second to say what we're thankful for, okay? I'll start. I'm thankful for my beautiful daughters. You are pure joy." Jacob looked at Sadie and Tabitha with warmth in his eyes. "I'm so thankful for mercy . . . second chances and new beginnings. I could go on and on."

Jacob turned to Sadie who sat to his right.

"I'm thankful for my family, and I'm thankful that we have more than enough." She turned her dark brown eyes to Samuel.

Gabriel raised his eyebrows and wondered if there was something brewing between Sadie and Samuel.

"Well, I'm thankful for being an honorary member of this family." Samuel smiled. "I'm thankful for health and a job that I love." Samuel pushed his sleeves up on his forearms as he buttered a biscuit.

"I guess I'm thankful for all that stuff too. I'm also thankful for being accepted. It hasn't always been that way for me. My grandma used to say I'm a lot to handle." Freddie raised his eyebrows and nodded as everyone chuckled and assured him sarcastically that *couldn't* be the case.

"I think we've all felt that way at one time or another, like we didn't belong. You belong here, Freddie," Jacob said as he took another biscuit. "Billy?"

The dark-haired, bearded brother looked up from his food, his eyes red and his long black hair pushed behind his ears. "I'm thankful for lots of things. I don't know, for starters, I'm thankful to be alive." He stared at the candle burning in front of him. "I'm thankful to be here . . . to be with you all. Forgiveness is all around this table. I guess if a family is known for that, that's a good thing. I'm also thankful for these sweet potatoes! Tabitha, what did you put in them? They can't be legal."

"Why, thank you. Maybe becoming a wife has helped me learn a little of this cooking thing. I guess it's my turn now," Tabitha said as she wiped her mouth. "I'm thankful for a life full of adventure and discovery. I'm thankful for a strong and courageous man who lets me be me." She put her hand on Gabriel's thigh. "I'm so thankful for life in The River. There was a time when I wondered if this was the life for me . . . if I was really meant to be here. I kept thinking I was missing something. I don't think that for a second now. My heart is full."

Gabriel noticed all eyes on him.

"My turn, huh? I'm thankful to be home. I'm thankful for the years in Kansas, but it's good to be home." He chuckled to himself as he continued. "My life looked quite a bit different just a few years ago. I was alone, working in the supply room of a five-and-dime. Now I'm in Colorado, spending my life at The River, married to the girl who is beyond even what my heart could dream, with people I love." Gabriel felt his eyes well with tears as he spoke. "I don't deserve any of this. I also want to say that . . ." He cleared his throat. "Sorry, guys. You know how easily the tears come with me. I'm thankful for those years with Ezra." He noticed tears springing in several other eyes. "I miss his cinnamon rolls. I miss the smell of that pipe. Jacob, you need to start smoking or something." Gabriel laughed and wipes his eyes. "I miss our talks. Once again, The River sent me a lifesaver." Gabriel reached for his glass of tea and raised it in the air. "Here's to the memory of Ezra Buchanan."

They clinked their glasses together.

Sadie spoke up. "Okay, name your favorite Ezra saying."

"'Sweet cinnamon!'" Freddie said with a grin.

"How about, 'It's good to remember what's good to remember,'" Gabriel said.

Sadie jumped in. "I know. I know. 'It's all in how ya look at it.'" She tried to make her voice deep with his slow Southern drawl.

Jacob spoke up. "One of my favorites is, 'I ain't who I once was, I ain't who I'm supposed to be yet, but I'm on my way and livin', and that's good.'"

Gabriel smiled as memories came rushing back. "He had an amazing way with words, but the thing that made Ezra great was not what he said, but what he did. He served in obscurity, never complained, was always so grateful, and he was always ready to lift someone up. His joy was . . . it was just complete and contagious. I wish everyone had the gift of rooming next door to him. I'm so glad it was me."

"You might be onto something," Jacob said.

"Onto what?"

"That everyone should have the gift of spending time with Ezra. Maybe we should write down a book of memories, you know, things he said and did. That is one way we could keep Ezra's legacy alive."

Tabitha piped up excitedly. "We could have an Ezra guide school, or even a mentor program, to help people through life. Look around the room, guys. We've all gone through some dark valleys. When we lost Mom . . . Ezra was there. He didn't always have the answers, but he always shared our tears. We could help people with what we are learning."

"The Ezra Buchanan Guide Center," Jacob said as he motioned with his hand. "Has a ring to it!"

Everyone nodded and commented in agreement.

"Okay, I think now is as good a time as any," Jacob declared to everyone. "Gabriel and Tabitha, I have something for you. I'll be right back."

They looked at each other and shrugged as they cleared the table after the feast.

Tabitha looked at Sadie. "Any clue?"

Sadie motioned to zip her mouth.

"Samuel? Do you know anything?"

He did the same.

"Freddie! Oh, Freddie!"

"Don't come over here; you know I can't keep secrets."

"I've got pie, Freddie," Tabitha singsonged as she held an apple pie.

Freddie stuck his fingers in his ears. "La-la-la-la!"

Right then Jacob walked in the door.

Tabitha's jaw dropped.

Gabriel jumped out of his chair and walked over in disbelief. There, draped across Jacob's arms, lay a beautiful

Siberian husky puppy. It had the most brilliant white and silver fur and ice-blue eyes.

Gabriel went over and tussled the fur of the adolescent pup as it licked his hands. "Hey, boy! Hey there! He's amazing. Is he ours?"

Jacob nodded. "All yours. It's been too long since Rio was running around here. I figured it was time you two had a kid anyway."

"Dad!" Tabitha slapped her father's shoulder.

Jacob pretended to wince. "What? I'm just saying!"

"Those eyes are breathtaking," Tabitha swooned as she stroked the pup's back.

"What should we call him?" Gabriel asked.

Tabitha pursed her lips. "Hmm . . . how about . . . Buchanan?"

Gabriel took the pup from Jacob and buried his face in the soft fur. "Buchanan. I like that. I like that a lot. We can call him 'B' for short."

They all sat around the fireplace taking turns doting over the canine and enjoying percolator coffee. Tabitha got slices of pie and served them up.

"Here you go, everyone, hot apple pie and ice cream. Gabriel, I think this is your best one yet." Gabriel spoke to himself.

"A man who bakes pies? It just doesn't get any better! Thank you!" Tabitha swooned as she took her piece.

"Well, you can thank Ezra. I watched him one day and wrote down his recipe the best I could."

After everyone had scraped their plates, Tabitha cleared her throat.

"So, Dad, you had a gift for us, and actually, Gabriel and I wanted to give you a little something." Tabitha handed him a small box wrapped in newspaper.

Jacob looked surprised. "What's that?" He shook it and put it up to his ear.

"Just open it, Dad," Tabitha said impatiently.

He sniffed it and then held it toward the dog. "Can you tell what that is, Buchanan?"

"Daddy!"

"Okay, okay," Jacob said, laughing.

He tore the old paper off and opened the small cardboard box. He pulled out an infant-sized life vest. He furrowed his brow as he studied it. "I'm confused."

Gabriel wrapped his arm around Tabitha, enjoying the surprise. "You're going to need it."

"For what?" Jacob said in exasperation.

Tabitha casually said, "Oh, when you babysit your first grandchild."

The news didn't register at first. Then Jacob's eyebrows rose and his eyes widened. He jumped up and down and started dancing what looked like a Celtic celebration of some sort. The others started clapping and laughing hysterically.

Jacob kept chanting as he danced. "I'm going to be a grandpa! I'm going to be a grandpa! I'm going to have a grandson!"

Tabitha laughed. "We don't know if it's a boy yet, Dad."

"Well, just a guess!" He threw his arms in the air. "Ha-ha! I'm going to be a grandpa!"

He ran over and picked his daughter up and hugged her tight.

"This is amazing. So amazing. I'm so happy." He let her down and went to Gabriel. "Congratulations, son." Jacob pulled him in and gave him a bear hug, lifting the young man's feet off the ground.

Jacob said it well: "Best Thanksgiving ever. Best Thanksgiving ever."

25

The Marble and
the King of Hearts

December 1977, Sunday, 6:50 a.m.

"I love you. I'll be back this afternoon," Gabriel said, feeling content. Standing at her side of the bed, he leaned over and kissed her tired forehead.

She rolled over and moaned. "It's a holiday. Where are you going at this hour?" She rubbed her eyes and looked at the clock that showed six fifty a.m.

"I just need some time."

"Everything okay?" She squinted as she looked into his eyes to see if there was anything behind his departure.

"Yes, of course. I'm going to the Cathedral. I'll be back before dinner."

She pulled his head down to hers and kissed his scruffy cheek.

Gabriel went to the back door and grabbed his black pea-coat, twirled his gray wool scarf around his neck, and pulled his army-green knit cap down over his hair. Before getting in his Jeep, he made his way down to the water's edge to breathe the damp, cold air. The gentle flow bubbled through the quiet canyon with a relentless peace. He took one glove off, stooped down, and dipped his hand in the frigid water. The early-morning mist hovered over the water as the glow of the dawn just started spilling into the gorge. His favorite part of the day was the awakening of morning. It meant new possibilities, a fresh start. Gabriel got in the Jeep and headed south.

After parking the Jeep off the road, he hiked for thirty minutes or so, carrying an old leather messenger bag and a small digging spade. He took the right fork on the trail and came through the last patch of trees to his familiar haunt, the Cathedral of the Sun. His pulse livened as he saw the large monolith and heard the roar of The River in the distance below. A little winded, he looked to the tops of the trees and felt the sun now peeking over the ridge. He heard the polyrhythmic melodies of a few songbirds in the trees and the occasional squirrel or chipmunk that darted about at the sound of his boots. He made his way to the base of the Cathedral to see his father's gravestone. Just a few yards to his right, his eyes lay hold of another important etched gravestone.

Ezra Buchanan
Faithful Friend to All
Forever in The River
1894–1975

Gabriel spoke aloud as he lowered his leather satchel from his shoulder and set it on the ground next to the small shovel.

"I brought something for each of you. I know you already know this, but there is another Clarke on the way. I'm going to be a dad. Can you believe it?" Gabriel smiled and talked like they were right in front of him. "It's a bit surreal, ya know? Taking care of a little one, I can't even imagine. I'm already torn up just thinking about it."

Gabriel opened the weathered bag and pulled out a small pouch. "Dad, remember when I came to visit you on your birthday? I found one of our marbles . . . well, Rio found it." He opened the pouch and pulled out the large aggie to take one more look, almost as if he was showing it to them. "I still can't believe it stayed there all those years." He dropped it back in the pouch. He took the digging spade, and directly centered between the two headstones, he dug a hole about eighteen inches deep. He set the pouch down in gently. "I wanted to leave this here with you. I have all the rest of them. I just want you to know I'll never forget what you did for Jacob and Billy, and how your story lives on in me, and . . . your soon-to-be grandchild. I'll do my best to never let you down." Gabriel wiped his moist eyes. He turned his attention to Ezra's place of rest. "Ezra, I miss you. You connected me to The River like no other. I'm forever in your debt, old friend." He reached into the bag and pulled out a playing card . . . a King of Hearts. "Whenever I play, I think of you taking all our money. You really were the king of hearts, Ezra. You always gave yourself away. You showed us how to have grace and dignity in the middle of great sorrow and adversity. Rather than giving way to your tears and becoming bitter . . . you planted them . . . you planted them in The River. You let The River turn them into joy. Joy from sorrow, that's how I remember you. I love you, wise friend." Gabriel set the card down into the hole. As he began to scoop the soft clay back into the hole, he wept.

The sun was in full view now, reflecting brilliantly in the dewy earth and the reddish canyon walls. Gabriel leaned back against the Cathedral rock and cushioned his head with the empty messenger bag. He watched as the occasional cloud floated by, hiding the sun's rays. His jubilation at the triumph of his son or daughter coming into the world stood valiantly in his heart as the waves of grief rolled in, breaking on his tired mind. He knew it would never fully leave. He was starting to understand that the joy was even more beautiful when standing on the shoulders of suffering. Scenes from his life began to flood in.

Breakfast at the Cartwright farm . . .

Riding the tractor with Tabitha . . .

Climbing the tree at the pond . . .

Buying marbles from the magic river marble man . . .

His wedding day . . .

Crying with Billy at Millie's grave . . .

Mrs. Collingsworth . . .

Rio saving his life from that snake . . .

Playing marbles with his father . . .

As he stared at the blue sky, it appeared to ripple, then some clouds started to rush together forming what appeared to be foaming white water. The scene cut to him guiding a raft that bucked ferociously in The River. In the front were two men. The white water sprayed Gabriel's face as he struggled to rudder the raft with his paddle. The two men turned around. It was his father on the left, just as he remembered him, in his early twenties! On the right, Ezra, who appeared younger than the last time he saw him! John and Ezra smiled and laughed as they paddled vigorously.

"Isn't this fantastic, Gabriel? What a day!" His father sounded overjoyed.

"I didn't remember it being like this! Yee-haw!" Ezra shouted.

Gabriel shook the water from his face. "Can you tell me what's going on here?"

"What do you mean, son? We are running The River!" John's husky voice echoed in the canyon as the waters calmed down.

A hawk screeched high overhead.

"We are getting ready to run some of the biggest waters you've ever seen. Yes, sir. You are going to love this." Ezra pulled his paddle in for a rest.

"What are you talking about? Where are we?" Gabriel looked all around the vast canyon. The walls were so high he could not see the top. The River so long he couldn't see the end in either direction. The water was crystal blue and the cliffs a deep gray. The trees were the richest shades of green, and the rocks on the banks sparkled like gems.

"There are a few things I want you to know, Gabriel. No matter how hard it gets, you're never alone." His father scooted closer to him on the raft.

"Great things are in store for you, Gabriel; it's been

planned for you since the beginning," Ezra said with wonder in his eyes as he pointed at Gabriel.

"There's always more going on than meets the eye. Listen to the waters. They will bring you people, people you can help," Ezra said.

"Remember, your covenant with Tabitha points to something far greater than you. It transcends your preferences. It should bring honor to her and to the ways of The River. Laying your life down for others, that's the way of The River. Oh, and by the way, it's a boy," his father said.

"I think Ezra would be a good name!" The old man laughed.

"Oh no, John is a much stronger name, old-timer!"

Gabriel tried to take in all they were saying.

"Always remember, Gabriel, with The River, it's always new. There's always a new beginning. It's never too late, for anyone. We all make mistakes. Once you're in The River, the old has gone and the new has come. Have courage and lead. You were meant to lead. So live! Live with hope! I'm proud of you, son. Always remember, we Clarkes, we were made for The River! Now let's make history!"

The old man reached over and started to tighten Gabriel's life vest.

"I think you're ready for the Big Water now. Make history, son." Ezra smiled as he and John spun around to face downstream.

Gabriel felt the water rise and the raft speed up. He looked ahead to notice the water spilling over a gorge and out of view. As the raft entered the thunderous mist, John and Ezra turned around one last time.

"See you on the other side!" they shouted in unison.

The sound of the impending waterfall was deafening. John and Ezra disappeared in the mist. The raft lunged forward . . .

A new voice entered. "Gabriel. Gabriel. You okay?"

"Hold on! Hold on!" Gabriel, startled and completely out of breath, looked up to see Jacob and Billy.

"Gabriel. It's just us. Looks like you had the same idea we did," his father-in-law said calmly as he let go of Gabriel's shoulder.

It took Gabriel just a second to get his bearings.

"I must have fallen asleep," he said as he sat up in the dirt.

The two men sat down beside him, one on either side. After a few moments of silence, Jacob spoke up. "This is a sacred place."

Then Billy. "I come here a lot . . . you know . . . to thank your dad."

They sat in the quiet, staring ahead.

Gabriel rubbed his face, still feeling odd. "You guys aren't going to believe the dream I just had."

"Try me," Jacob responded.

Gabriel grabbed a pen and journal out of his satchel and began to write as fast as he could.

"Once I get it straight in my head, I'll share it."

"Do you think God speaks to us in dreams?" Billy asked.

"It's hard to know what is God and what isn't sometimes, that's for sure. I would like to know His mind on things." Gabriel took his finger and began to write something in the dirt.

New Beginnings

Gabriel continued, "I have to believe, though, if we're hungry to hear Him, He'll let us know. Somehow . . . some way, He'll speak. Maybe through people, through dreams, through circumstances, through His mystery, and we'll know. Hey, Fielding brothers, I want you to know something."

"What's that?" Jacob asked with a questioning look.

"It's okay. We're okay."

Nothing more needed to be said in that moment. Gabriel got up first and offered each of his hands to the other two. The three guides stood over the gravestones of their heroes thinking about all they were thankful for. Second chances, new relationships, and a new child, all in the current of The River. Gabriel picked up his leather satchel and threw it over his shoulder.

"Gentlemen, it's up to us now. What will you do with your new beginning? As for me . . . I'd like to make history."

Epilogue

October 8, 2012, 9:20 a.m.

It was my last day with Gabriel at The River. I needed to leave for the airport before dawn the next morning. I almost didn't want to. Being with this man out in the wilderness opened me up at the deepest level. The River saw right through me. I couldn't hide a thing. I had seen a river before, but this time, I experienced it. I felt the water's touch. I heard the water's voice. I really saw The River's power and beauty. Before this trip, I never really knew I needed forgiveness. I don't think I'd ever been truly honest with anyone until Gabriel Clarke. He didn't judge me. He just led me through to a place of truth.

The hike was more challenging than I thought. We came to the fork and went left. It was a cool, damp, and cloudy late morning.

"The Cathedral is to the right. We'll stop there on the way back." His low, gravelly voice sounded strong and reverent.

"Okay . . . right behind you."

The sound of the thundering falls rose with every slog of my boots. We arrived at a clearing. He took his backpack off. I followed his lead.

"Come with me," he said as we walked to the edge of the ridge. "That's Firewater Gorge."

The falls, the spray, the rock formations created a dazzling display of nature. "Wow. It's even more magnificent than I imagined."

"Grab on to this tree," he instructed with his hand on a broad fir tree.

I did.

"This is the tree that I clung to fifty-six years ago now."

I felt hollow as I considered what he'd carried with him his entire life. The terrifying scene from that tree must have played in his mind a million times.

Gabriel scrambled down the hill to the water's edge next to the falls. I followed carefully. He stood with his back to the water as I arrived. He pointed over my shoulder to a tree that was now behind me. I turned to see the deep etching in the spruce, the symbol of Ama-Woya, the sign of the scar named "mercy" on Jacob, the symbol of freedom, and the symbol of The River.

"We believe that's the original one, the sign she carved to commemorate her freedom. Life brings many scars, many tears, Blake. The River meets us in the tears and washes our scars. The ashes of our brokenness and grief will one day give way to displays of love and beauty. It's written in the scars."

Gabriel ran his hand over the moss-stained tree carving. He turned to The River and pointed to a giant boulder in the current next to the bank where the waters poured around it powerfully.

"Is that where it happened?" I asked.

He nodded.

"I still miss him." He cupped his hands to his mouth like a megaphone and shouted, "I love you! In . . . The . . . River! In . . . The . . . River!" His voice seemed to carry all the way to the top of the canyon ridge. He was uninhibited by my presence or whether I would understand such a thing. I was so moved by this battle cry . . . this cry of love . . . this cry of devotion.

I stooped down and leaned over the bank to touch the water. Something happened as I did. I've never seen visions. I've had dreams, of course, but when the mist of the waterfall hit my face and I felt the water push against my hand, I had the most vivid scenes flash into my mind's eye. They terrified me. They probably only lasted fractions of a second, but they are forever etched in my mind and heart.

My family, Sarah, Jake, Lily, and Dylan, were in a raft by themselves. The raft was spinning. Sarah was doing her best to control it in the raging water but to no avail. They were careening toward a massive waterfall. I could read the kids' lips. They were looking at me, shouting, "Daddy! Daddy!" but I couldn't hear them. The looks of terror on their faces broke my heart. I started banging on the window of my BMW and yanking on the door handle. I was locked in my luxury car on the bank watching the most beautiful gifts of my life struggle and then disappear.

I jerked my hand out of the water and shook my head.

I was gasping with anxiety. I felt like I couldn't breathe. I stood back up to my feet, and Gabriel looked at me as if he knew what I'd seen.

"Let's go. One more place."

I couldn't shake the feeling of what just happened. We climbed back up the steep hill, grabbing small trees and setting our feet in the embedded rocks. We hiked back the way we came to the fork and took a left. After another strenuous thirty-minute haul, we came to the place I will never forget.

"Welcome to the Cathedral of the Sun, Blake."

As I approached the massive rock, the sun broke through the clouds. It absolutely was nature's cathedral. The rock spires rose mightily into the sky. I felt small in their shadow. I walked with Gabriel over to the base, and we set our backpacks down. I saw the gravestones. I felt an amazing connection to history, to greatness, and to my new friend's story as I looked at the names.

John W. Clarke
1928–1956
Forever in The River

I thought of the legacy of this man. He was a true hero . . . a legend. After a few moments I took a couple of steps over and gazed at the next one.

Ezra Buchanan
Faithful Friend to All
Forever in The River
1894–1975

I contemplated the selflessness of this gentle soul. How he led Gabriel through the most difficult times with timeless wisdom.

It was the next one that humbled me to the dust and caused my heart to sink.

Tabitha Fielding Clarke
Beloved Wife and Mother
The Canyon Princess
Forever in The River
1954–2010

I felt his presence as he joined me.

"I didn't know, Gabriel. I'm so sorry."

"We had thirty-six beautiful years together. We lived for each other and for The River." He knelt down on both knees, wiping debris from the stone as he continued. "She was so feisty, all the way up until the day the cancer won. She was still telling me to never stop living and to go for my dreams. She believed in me. Do you know what her last words to me were? 'You have to do the Top 10!' When I first met you in the airport, I was coming back from that trip. Every rapid of that trip was run in her honor. Oh . . . we had some rocky times too, but we never quit. We loved each other . . . forgave each other . . . through it all."

Gabriel wiped his eyes as he stood back up. He faced me. I felt like he saw my soul.

"I'd give anything . . . to have one more day, one more picnic under the falls, one more good night kiss, one more run of The River, one more *anything* with her. My Tabitha is gone, Blake. But yours . . ." He put his finger in my chest. ". . . Your Tabitha . . . is still here. What are you going to do about it? What are you going to give your life to? What are you going to run after? You still have a choice. Which path will you choose?"

His words lanced my heart, and I wept at the Cathedral of the Sun.

I loaded the last of my things into my car and shut the trunk. As Gabriel walked over from the lodge, a vintage faded yellow Range Rover Jeep rumbled into the drive. A thirty-something, blond-bearded outdoorsman jumped out as soon as it stopped.

"There he is!" The young man ran and embraced Gabriel.

"Blake! Come here!" the guide shouted. "I'd like you to meet John Ezra, my son. We call him J.E."

I extended my hand to have it nearly crushed by the rock-solid man. He was the spitting image of his father.

"Nice to meet you, Blake."

"You too. So are you a guide as well?" I asked.

Gabriel answered before his son could.

"The best." He wrapped his arm around his shoulder. "He and I are getting ready to run some big water over the next few days. There's nothing better than having your son become your best friend." He looked at his son with eyes full of pride. "You ready to make history?"

"Let's do it," J.E. said confidently.

"Have a safe trip back, my friend." Gabriel extended his strong and weathered hand and pulled me in for hug.

"Gabriel, I can't thank you enough."

"Listen, you're welcome anytime. I have a great idea. Bring your whole family! We'll show them the time of their lives." He opened his eyes wide and smiled.

"I hope I get a chance to take you up on that, friend."

"Well, if you do, I'll have to share some of the most amazing miracles that our family has experienced on The River. They'll blow your mind," he said through that comforting, crazed grin.

"Nice to meet you, J.E."

"You too."

I climbed in my car. As I was getting ready to shut my door, he called my name one last time.

"Blake."

I turned.

"Go make history."

———❦———

It was dusk as I pulled into the long drive of our small farm back in Tennessee. My heart jumped out of my chest as I saw a couple of bikes lying on the side of the drive and her SUV in front of the garage. Out of the corner of my eye, Dylan came sprinting from the side yard carrying his firefly net.

"Daddy's home! Daddy's home!" He grabbed onto my leg like a little capuchin monkey. "I caught eleventeen fireflies, Dad!"

Lily came skipping around from the back of the garage carrying her glow-in-the-dark hulahoop around her waist. Her smile was electric.

Jake was sitting under a large maple tree in an old Adirondack chair with his headphones on. He took one off.

"Where you been?"

I looked to the front porch of the house, and there was Sarah standing in the twilight. Her arms were folded. Her hair was pulled back in a ponytail and she wore my favorite faded jeans and sweater. Her face looked as beautiful as ever, but tired from crying. My heart melted at the sight of her. There was more love in her eyes than anger, which surprised me.

I spent a few moments with the kids, asking them about the fun they'd had at Grandma's and such.

"Guys, I need to talk to Mom for a few minutes. Then maybe we'll all go get some dinner, okay?"

"I'm making dinner. It'll be ready in about thirty minutes." She leaned up against the support beam on the porch. Her voice sounded kind but distant.

"Would you walk with me for a minute?"

She threw the dish towel over her shoulder and strolled by my side over to the large tire swing on the edge of the property.

The first words out of my mouth brought both of us heavy tears.

"I'm so sorry. I'll do whatever it takes. Please tell me we aren't over. Please tell me you'll give me a chance. You are the love of my life. You're my best friend. I've been chasing everything that's wrong. I want you. I want the kids. I don't know how I let myself wander. I just . . ."

My words came out like a machine gun until she stopped me.

"It hurts so deep, Blake. I can't even explain it. I'm so angry. But I know it's not just you. I've shut you out. We need help, Blake . . . we need help. We need a new beginning."

"Whatever it takes, Sarah. Whatever it takes, I'll do it."

I dropped to my knees.

"I love you, Sarah. With all my heart . . . I love you."

She knelt down slowly, and we embraced in the tear-soaked dirt under the maple tree with the tire swing. In a moment of the greatest love and grace I'd ever known on this earth, my bride sat next to me for dinner that night.

Sarah and I have been on the richest and most glorious journey. It's been a painful road, but pain toward healing, like surgery.

We've dug up the bones, but we're giving them a proper burial. It's a burial in The River, so to speak.

It's been a journey toward each other. Grace and forgiveness are winning the battle over judgment and condemnation. We have been given another chance, and we are not wasting a second of it. I'm giving my life to something greater now. No more empty pursuits. Relationships . . . in the end . . . they are the only things that matter.

When your life collides with someone like Gabriel Clarke, you're never the same. I want to live a life like that . . . a life of unexplainable purpose and love in the face of fear and tragedy.

Sarah and I are taking the kids out to Big Water Adventures this year. I want them to meet Gabriel and John

Ezra. There is so much more of his story I want to hear. I can't wait to show them what I saw, teach them what I learned, and hope beyond hope that the ways of The River get in them too. I hope we'll see you there. If not, you can be sure I'll write about it. It's important to share our stories. It helps us know we aren't alone.

Don't forget the words of my friend Gabriel Clarke, "We are all made for The River."

Reading Group Guide

1. How did Gabriel grow and change from the young man at the beginning of his adventures on The River to the older man we see in the story with Blake?
2. What did the Ama-Woya's scar symbolize?
3. How did Gabriel's relationship with Jacob help the healing process of grieving his dad's death?
4. How did hearing the words his friends used to describe him on the Stones of Remembrance affect Gabriel? Is there someone in your life who needs to hear similar words of encouragement? What word would you add about yourself?
5. Billy deals with a tremendous amount of grief and shame. Did you relate to his struggle?
6. Gabriel tells Blake, "When I come to The River, I'm actually the truest version of myself. I think that's because I

realize it's not about me." What do you think he wanted Blake to understand about this statement?

7. Why do think it took so long for Gabriel to truly share his heart and struggles with Tabitha?

8. How did the unpredictability, danger, and beauty of The River impact each of the characters?

9. What do you think Gabriel learned about himself when he went home to Kansas?

10. What part of Ezra's story was the most meaningful to you?

11. What do you think was the most significant moment for Blake during his time on The River with Gabriel?

12. Ezra often said, "It's good to remember what's good to remember." What does that phrase mean to you?

Acknowledgments

It is an insurmountable task to cover the list of all those who have shaped us along the journey. The writing of each book is certainly a journey for me. I'm forever indebted to so many who have lifted me with encouragement, guided me with wisdom, covered me with prayer, and changed me with love.

To Leah—my high school sweetheart, my best friend and one true love. You make me a better human. When this book releases we will have celebrated twenty-one years of marriage. I can't wait to see where life takes us in the next twenty-one!

To the most amazing kids a guy could dream of being a dad to:

To Micah—my firstborn son. You are a leader and a rock. I'm so proud of you. You have such character and you use your strength for good.

To Maisie—my beautiful princess. You are so kind and patient. Your poise and great sense of humor are such gifts!

To Wyatt—you light up the room everywhere you go! Keep singing, dancing, and kickboxing!

I Love you guys beyond words!

To my sister Joy, brother-in-law Mike, Moriah, Mikaela, and Brooke—I love you all. Your perseverance is inspiring. Joy, I'm so proud of you.

To my brother-in-law Lt. Colonel Scott Harris, Leighann, Jessica, Scott, and Justin—we love that you are so close now. Let's get some tacos! Scott, we are all deeply grateful for your service to our country.

To my cousin Dan Lamb—I treasure your friendship, man. You are one of the most talented dudes I know. Thank you for all the rides to the airport and for being such a champion.

To my cousin Steve Lamb—you are an inspiration to us all. As I type this you are still recovering from that car accident, but I know when the book releases, you'll be going full steam again. Your strength and perseverance is building courage in all of us.

To Aunt Barbara, Aunt Kathy, Aunt Suzi, Aunt Carol and family—thank you for all your encouraging words and support.

To Aunt Becki—we love you and are thankful for you. Thanks for always cheering us on.

To the best in-laws, Janis and Mike Evans—we are so grateful for your love and the way you love your grandchildren. You are always in our thoughts and prayers.

To my friend and agent, Kurt "Swami" Beasley. I'm so

thankful for your counsel and friendship. The talks on the porch have brought comfort and clarity on the journey. Lady Beasley, thank you for your generous hospitality and, of course, the smoothies.

To Whitney Smith—your assistance in the office has been invaluable. Thank you for everything you have done to take care of the unseen details.

To Jody Guthrie, Director of The River Education Initiative—You are so inspiring! You are a brilliant light as you give selflessly to all the beautiful kids you teach. Thank you for seeing what could be and for working so tirelessly to build this dream. You are a living example of "The River Life."

To my pastors and mentors, Todd Mullins, Tom Mullins, and John Maxwell—what a gift to call you friends and mentors. I'm forever indebted to you for your investment in my life. What a gift to be able to flourish in the overflow of your faithfulness and ministry.

To my CF brothers, James Duvall, Adam Baldwin, Jay Boykin, Brian Taylor, Steven Robertson, Brad Parsley, Shaun Blakeney, Tim Moore, Matt Pilot, and the entire team—it is an honor to serve with you guys, and an even greater privilege to call you friends.

To Daisy Hutton and the Thomas Nelson/Harper-Collins team—thank you for believing in my stories and helping me take them far wider than I ever could. I count it a great privilege to work alongside the best!

To my fantastic editors, Ami McConnell and Nicci Jordan Hubert—you ladies are rock stars. I can't thank you enough for your patience with this sophomore author.

Thank you for making me a better writer and for helping this story to be as compelling as possible. I am in your debt.

To all the friends near and far who champion my work— I am humbled and grateful.

An excerpt from *The River*

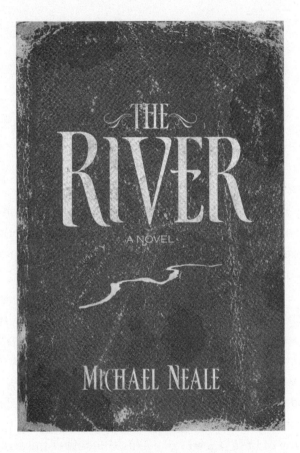

Prologue

Every now and then, you have an encounter with someone who simply changes your life. A conversation or interaction so profound, it seems otherworldly. You can't get his (or her) story out of your head and heart.

It's hard to explain how powerful stories can resonate within us on many levels, but it's often because of the way they speak with passion, heartache, or even joy. Maybe it's the way they unknowingly reach into our heart of hearts with their words.

I don't think these encounters happen by chance. I think there is a reason, although we will never understand the full weaving of life's tapestry of events this side of the eternal. I have had such an encounter with someone. It moved me to my core, so much so that I had to share it with you. I'll keep sharing it as long as I have breath. For the next few pages, I'd like you to grab a cup of coffee—or a root beer float—and sit down and let me tell you about a conversation I had with a man named Gabriel Clarke.

It all began when I was traveling back to Nashville from the West Coast. My first flight from LAX landed in Denver at about 6:30 p.m. on a Thursday night, when things at DIA were slowing down a bit. I was feeling exhausted after two days of countless meetings, a lack of rest (I don't sleep well away from home), and the tiring travel.

I'm not sure what it is about planes, but the only way I can describe it is that flying makes me feel stale, grimy, and in need of a teeth cleaning. I got off of my first flight from Los Angeles and approached the monitor to see which gate was handling my connecting flight.

According to my itinerary, I had about fifty minutes until my flight to Nashville took off. The monitor said otherwise. Like a deer staring into oncoming headlights, I stood fixated at the monitor, hoping my glare would supernaturally change the DELAYED message to BOARDING.

Unfortunately, that did not happen. After a quick visit to the restroom, I made the trek to my new gate, dodging the carts carrying the old folks and doing my best to ignore the annoying beeps. When I arrived, I discovered that my flight was not delayed—it was *canceled* due to mechanical issues with the aircraft.

There wasn't much I could do except queue up with a line of agitated passengers waiting to speak with the gate agent. In a very unsympathetic and "get over it" tone, she explained that my only option was to reschedule on a different flight leaving at 10:50 p.m.

I did some quick calculations. With the time change, this would put me in my own bed on our small farm forty-five minutes outside of Nashville at about three a.m. Oh joy. I *love* going home, just not in the middle of the night when I'm tiptoeing around like a burglar, trying to keep our chocolate labs from waking the kids.

I took a deep breath and resigned myself to my fate. I had a three-and-a-half-hour rendezvous with the C Concourse in Denver, there was no way around it. I hunted for a quiet corner where I could spend some time reading and listening to music. It was a rare opportunity for downtime, so I figured I'd make the most of it.

About eight gates down, I found an entire section where the lights were dim, the hanging flat-screen TVs were turned off, and the gates were closed. There wasn't a soul in sight. I looked for the best spot and claimed a section of seating in the back corner, next to the windows that looked out over the tarmac. I called my wife and kids to say good night and break the news that I wouldn't see them until the morning.

After we said our good-byes, I immediately reached for my iPod, plugged in my earphones, and shut out the world by listening to my favorite movie scores. I had a spy novel I'd started on the flight from LA, so I pulled the oversized paperback out of my backpack, propped my feet up on the chair across from me, and began reading. After ten pages, though, my solitude and bliss came to an abrupt end.

Out of the corner of my eye, I saw a large character moving toward me. *Who in the world is heading all the way over here? Surely it's not someone I know from home.* My thoughts were running a mile a minute. Sure enough, this man plopped down two seats from me and opened a canvas bag that looked to be filled with enough camping and hiking gear to scale the Himalayas.

I couldn't believe it. Of all the places in the airport, why would he sit down right next to me? I ignored him, burying my head in my book, but he kept going through his canvas bag, checking his equipment and carrying on a one-sided conversation with himself.

I turned my music up, sighed loudly, and returned to my book, trying to send a message that I wanted to be left alone. Out of the corner of my eye, I noticed that he kept looking over at me again and again. I could tell he was itching for conversation, so I looked up from my book and gave Mountain Man a halfhearted grin.

He was at least six feet tall and built like an Australian rugby player. A long, shaggy beard with disheveled dirty-blond hair poured out from under his army-green knit cap. If I had to guess his age, I would say that he was probably in his midfifties. Dressed in a worn-thin plaid flannel shirt with rolled-up sleeves and khaki shorts, he wore large hiking boots with thick thermal socks bunched around his ankles. His skin was weathered and tan, his eyes were crystal blue, and his worn face was lined with wrinkles. He looked like he'd just stepped out of a Discovery Channel documentary.

The older man looked at me and said something. I couldn't understand him because of the cranked-up music playing in my ears, so I pulled out my earphones. "Sorry, man, I couldn't hear you. What was that?"

"Heading home or away?"

Not a very deep question. "I'm heading home," I said, hoping my three-word reply would send a hint that I didn't want to be bothered.

He would not be deterred. "Me too. I've been gone for over three months. I'm ready for my own bed." He slouched in his chair and leaned back, staring at the ceiling. I thought maybe our conversation was over, meaning I could get back to my book and music in peace.

Instead, he looked over again. "How long until your flight leaves?"

I knew now that I should just give in, so I closed my book and set it on my lap.

"I have until ten thirty," I said, and I told him what happened with the canceled flight to Nashville. He told me he was early for his red-eye to the East Coast.

From there, we exchanged the typical small talk:

"Where are you from?"

"Where are you going?"

"Weather has been unpredictable, huh?"

All the usual stuff. But with guys, an introductory conversation wouldn't be complete unless you ask, "What do you do?"

I always hate talking about what I do, but it's part of the man language. We feel we can tell a lot about a person by what they do for a living.

So I plunged in. "What do you do for a living?" I asked curiously.

He hedged a little bit. "Well, I like the outdoors a lot, you know." He smiled and looked at me, comfortable with the awkward pause.

"Well, what about this three-month trip you were on? Was it work related, or just R & R?"

"Oh no," he said through a chuckle. "Not much R & R on this trip. I just finished running *National Geographic*'s Top Ten Most Dangerous and Beautiful Rivers in the World. Five continents, nineteen thousand miles, a couple of near-death experiences, some serious wildlife, tons of new friends, and the time of my life." He looked over at me out of the corner of his eye. "It was outrageous," he said with a bit of a crazed grin.

The conversation became riveting. I found out his name was Gabriel Clarke, a third-generation whitewater guide. For the next several hours, Gabriel regaled me with his life story—the legendary story of where he came from, the defining tragedy of his childhood, the triumph of where he was in life now, and what got him through. The way he energetically explained things, it was as if this was the first time he'd ever told anyone.

His passion was contagious, and by the time he was finished, I was thankful for the interruption that night in the Denver airport. What I'm about to tell you is his story as he told it to me. If you're anything like me, or others who've heard Gabriel's story, then you'll never forget it. You'll never be the same.

I know I'll never be the same—ever.

The story continues in The River . . .

About the Author

Author photo by Nashville Photography Group

Gifted writer, veteran performer, and masterful storyteller are all phrases used to describe Michael Neale. He's currently leading a live, multimedia concert event known as The River Experience, which immerses the audience in breathtaking film imagery and a world-class musical score. Michael resides in Palm Beach Gardens, Florida, with his wife, Leah, and their children, Micah, Maisie, and Wyatt.